HOW TO DELIVER A
TED TALK

Secrets of the World's
Most Inspiring Presentations

JEREMEY DONOVAN

New York Chicago San Francisco Athens London Madrid
Mexico City Milan New Delhi Singapore Sydney Toronto

1 2 3 4 5 6 7 8 9 0   QFR/QFR   1 9 8 7 6 5 4 3

ISBN   978-0-07-183159-8
MHID   0-07-183159-2

e-ISBN 978-0-07-182957-1
e-MHID   0-07-182957-1

Library of Congress Cataloging-in-Publication Data
Donovan, Jeremey.
   How to deliver a TED talk : secrets of the world's most inspiring presentations, revised and expanded new edition, with a foreword by Richard St. John and an afterword by Simon Sinek / Jeremey Donovan.
      pages cm
   ISBN 978-0-07-183159-8 (pbk. : alk. paper) –ISBN 0-07-183159-2 (alk. paper)
   1. Business presentations. 2. Public speaking. 3. Business communication. I. Title.
   HF5718.22.D66 2013
   658.4'52–dc23

                                                              2013025278

McGraw-Hill Education books are available at special quantity discounts to use as premiums and sales promotions or for use in corporate training programs. To contact a representative, please visit the Contact Us pages at www.mhprofessional.com.

CONTENTS

PART I
CONTENT

PART II
DELIVERY

PART III

DESIGN

PART IV

THE JOURNEY TO THE STAGE AND BEYOND

FOREWORD

Most forewords are dedicated to singing the praises of authors and their books. Jeremey and his book certainly deserve it! However, he felt that you would be better served if I shared with you the story behind my first TED Talk.[1] My passion is helping people succeed, so I am thrilled to oblige.

I have attended 20 TED Conferences, starting in 1994. It became my annual pilgrimage to see fascinating speakers and to be immersed in ideas worth spreading. For years I was strictly a listener, far too shy to talk to any of the big names. Back then, few people even knew the conference existed. When I said I was going to TED, the usual response was, "Ted who?"

Then in 1998 I'm on a plane on my way to TED, and in the seat next to me is a teenage girl. She came from a poor family, but she wanted to get somewhere in life, and she asked me, "What really leads to success?" Even though I had achieved a degree of success, I couldn't answer her question. I got off the plane, went to TED, and found myself standing in a room full of successful people in many different fields. Then it hit me. Why don't I ask them what helped them succeed and find out what really leads to success?

I got excited. I wanted to interview people. But then the self-doubt and shyness set in; why would these people want to talk to me? I'm not a famous journalist. I froze up, sweating, butterflies in my stomach, and slumped back against the wall. I was ready to stop the project before it even began, when who comes walking toward me but Ben Cohen, cofounder of Ben & Jerry's Ice Cream. I figured it was now or never, so I jumped out in front of him and blurted out,

"Ben, I'm working on this project. I don't even know what to ask you, but can you tell me what helped you succeed?" He says, "Sure, let's go for a coffee."

You would think that little success would have wiped out the fear. No way. For the first 300 interviews, the shyness, anxiety, and butterflies all came rushing back every time I approached someone. But it's all about practice, and now a thousand interviews later I'm not shy at all. If Oprah walked by, I'd jump into her arms.

At that point I had spent six years studying success and had a ton of useful information to share. But how? Just the thought of speaking in front of an audience made me shake. So I took a public speaking course. (Actually my wife took one first, and I copied her, which is how it usually works.) I go to this course every Monday night and push myself to stand up in front of a small group and then give a two-minute speech. The first week I was so scared I could hardly open my mouth. But after 12 weeks of practice the fear and shyness dissolved.

After the course I was still not a great speaker, but I could deliver a talk without shaking in my boots. I felt ready to start sharing my findings, with young people in particular, like the girl on the plane. I put together a two-hour PowerPoint presentation and gave some talks to small groups of high school students in their living rooms. Then as my confidence grew, I pushed myself to speak to hundreds of students in a high school auditorium.

Now it's 2004 and the next TED Conference is approaching. I wished to share my research with all the TEDsters who gave me interviews over the years. I e-mailed Chris Anderson, who took over TED in 2002, "Chris, I'm coming to Silicon Valley on business. Can I show you my research findings on success? It might make a good TED Talk." He very kindly meets me for breakfast at Buck's Diner in Woodside, and I go through my two-hour PowerPoint presentation. (Poor Chris!) He gave me great feedback—but no TED Talk.

Then a year later, in 2005, Chris sent out a notice saying they want to try some three-minute talks, in addition to the usual 18-minute ones, and to apply if you're interested. Instantly I responded, "Chris, remember that two-hour presentation I gave you in Buck's Diner? I can do it in three minutes." Chris: "In 180 seconds??? That's when your microphone gets cut off." Me: "You bet! Not a second over!" Chris: "OK. You're on. Good luck."

Now the pressure was on to reduce my talk from two hours to three minutes. I spent weeks cutting and revising, then practicing it hundreds of times. All the while those 180 seconds are looming over my head, ready to cut me off in midsentence. However, the three-minute enemy is actually a friend because it forces me to get to the heart of the content and be crystal clear.

Finally, I was sitting in the front row at TED, waiting to go on stage. I looked around and saw big names like Bill Gates and all these great speakers I really admire. The presenter before me was James Watson, Nobel Prize–winning codiscoverer of the DNA structure. You want to be nervous, try following him. I thought, what the hell am I doing here? Nobody wants to hear me. My anxiety increased; my stomach churned. I glanced down at a piece of paper in my hand where I've scribbled three reminders: 1. Have fun. 2. Keep smiling. 3. Richard Feynman. Why this great physicist? Because in his book *Surely You're Joking, Mr. Feynman*, he recounts how he calmed himself when he had to give a talk with Albert Einstein in the audience:

> *I remember very clearly seeing my hands shaking as I pulled out my notes from a brown envelope. But then a miracle occurred . . . the moment I start to think about the physics, and have to concentrate on what I'm explaining, nothing else occupies by mind—I'm completely immune to being nervous.*

As I sat there shaking, I reminded myself of that; then walking up onto the TED stage I'm concentrating 100 percent on my content and what I need to communicate. Everything else is shut out. My eyes make contact with audience members, but my mind is totally absorbed in what I'm saying. I look at the clock. Oh no! It's already running. The 180 seconds are ticking away. I flew through the talk as fast as I could—no pauses—no stopping—no waiting for laughter to subside—and I finished right on time. Whew! And that's the story behind my first TED Talk.

I want to leave you with a few pieces of advice that mirror what you will read in this book. First, forget about being a great speaker. Just go out there and do your best to spread your ideas. Speaking does not inspire people; content inspires people. Second, there are different strokes for different folks. Ken Robinson has his style, and I have mine. Be authentic and communicate the way you are off-stage. Third, stick to the script. If you have spent days, weeks, and sometimes months working on a speech, then do not throw it away and improvise on the spot. I have seen a number of speakers start ad-libbing, and it's always the worst part of their talk. And last, practice, practice, practice. It's the key to getting good at anything, including speaking. I've interviewed many great speakers. Not one was a "natural" speaker. They all practiced more than anyone else.

Jeremey prefers that I not praise his book, so to conclude my introduction let me just say this: When I received a copy of this book, I picked it up and quickly started underlining great ideas to help me deliver better talks. Now half of my bloody book is underlined! If you have an idea worth spreading, this book is worth reading.

–Richard St. John,
author of *The 8 Traits Successful People Have in Common: 8 to Be Great*

ACKNOWLEDGMENTS

At the November 2011 Toastmasters District 53 Fall Conference, I delivered an educational workshop entitled "Step-by-Step Guide to Delivering Exceptional Keynote Presentations" based on insights from my private study of TED Talks. I was shocked to discover there was surprisingly little cross-pollination between TED and Toastmasters. After the session, my Toastmasters friends gave me a mountain of constructive feedback and encouraged me to turn the workshop into a book. A few of the Toastmasters who have had a profound impact on this book include Joshua Reynolds, Grant DuBois, Nana Danso, Ryan Avery, Craig Valentine, Simone Morris, Sarah Goshman, Nicol Rupolo, Jane Shan, Eileen Murphy, and Tom Kobak.

A short, self-published version of this book was released on March 24, 2012. It was lovingly edited by my patient wife, Irene, who got much better grades than I did in English class. When I write, I define success as giving one copy to my daughter Emma and one to my son Ethan. When I gave Emma her copy, she said, "Dad . . . you wrote a pamphlet!" Through nothing more than dumb luck, my 100-page pamphlet began to get traction in the speaking community and spread from there.

As I was sitting in a coffee shop on January 28, 2013 in New York City preparing to give my "How to Deliver a TED Talk" talk to a group of educators, I received the following message in LinkedIn:

Jeremey, I am President of Whimsy Literary Agency and I have an editor who is interested in picking up your book. Please contact me to discuss. Thanks. Jackie Meyer.

Though my scam detector was on high alert, I spent a half an hour researching Jackie's background and quickly discovered that she is the real deal. Jackie became more than my agent; she is my trusted friend and advisor. With an hour to go before my presentation, I called Jackie, and she instantly connected me with McGraw-Hill editor Casey Ebro. Improbably, Casey agreed to come to the workshop I was holding that night. Though it may seem like a no-brainer, there are major trade-offs in moving from self-publishing to traditional publishing. I appreciate that few people are lucky enough to even have that choice. I made the decision because of my confidence in Casey; her unfathomable depth of knowledge about how people communicate convinced me that we could build a better book to inspire others to express their ideas worth spreading. I would like to come clean and admit that Jackie and Casey think I am a decent writer only because of PJ Dempsey's expert proofreading and editing skills.

The biggest differences between a self-published work and a professionally published book are quality and marketing. I am indebted to the following individuals on the McGraw-Hill team for the magic they create behind the scenes: Chelsea Van der Gaag, Ann Pryor, Mary Glenn, Ron Martirano, and Janice Race.

Finally, I would like to express my appreciation to the TED Conferences organization and to the speakers who have inspired me with their messages and their delivery. In particular, I am grateful to Richard St. John, Simon Sinek, Daniel Pink, and Becky Blanton for unveiling the TED speaking experience that you cannot see in the auditoriums or on the videos. Additionally, my thanks go to the following speakers for generously granting their permission to me to publish quotes from their amazing TED Talks: Joe Smith, Jill Bolte Talylor, Matt Cutts, Bunker Roy, Susan Cain, Salman Khan, Ken Robinson, Elizabeth Gilbert, Cameron Russell, Deb Roy, Jamie Oliver, Regena Thomashauer, Hans Rosling, Ric Elias, Amanda Palmer, Jane Chen, and Brené Brown.

Confessions of a TED Talk Addict

I still remember the day, back when I was eight years old, when I decided what I wanted to do for the rest of my life. It was a time before TED Talks, before the Internet, which made them a global phenomenon, even existed. In those days, the people who created electronics built them to last, and the people who purchased electronics cherished them. My family, like all the other families I knew, squeezed every ounce of life from our gadgets until the switches and fans and lights became so arthritic that even the electronics repairman pronounced them too far gone to resuscitate.

The piece of electronics I cherished most was the flip-style alarm clock in my parents' bedroom. If you have never seen one of these relics, then just imagine a flip pad with numbers on the pages. As one page falls down, it covers the previous number and reveals a new one. There was something both forbidding and magical about the clock. Though I was not allowed to touch it for fear of disrupting my parents' routine, I would sometimes sit on their bed waiting for the motor inside to move the gears that would cause the numbers to flip with a satisfying "click!"

1

And then one day tragedy struck. The motor whirred, but then the gears made an ominous grinding sound, and the flip page indicated that the last minute digit was stuck halfway between 6 and 7. I promised my parents that I did not touch it, and for once they believed me. Mindful of my unusual passion for this inanimate object, my mother gave me the alarm clock, a screwdriver, and one instruction, "Just don't plug it in after you take it apart, or you are likely to electrocute yourself." Ah, parents and their penchant for putting ideas into their children's heads . . .

As I dissected the alarm clock, I examined the wonders of the electrical and mechanical components inside. Fancying myself a skilled technician, I reassembled the machine with more than a few unintended modifications. When it was back together, there were still a few parts lying on the floor and a few more rattling away inside. Hoping to please my parents with my cleverness in fixing their treasured timekeeper, I plugged the clock into the wall. It started to smoke a little with the toxic smell of burning plastic, so I removed the plug from the wall socket before I did myself any real harm.

I knew in that moment that I wanted to be an engineer. You see, I was a quiet, introverted kid who lived in his head and didn't speak much. I figured that as an engineer I could have a rewarding career playing with gadgets. Best of all, I would not have to talk to anyone!

I'll save you the bits and bobs in between, but 14 years later my dream came true. I got to play with computers and manufacturing equipment as a newly minted semiconductor engineer in Silicon Valley. The only problem was that I hated my job. Though I was happy that I did not have to talk much, the integrated circuits I produced were many, many production steps upstream from the gadgets that human beings actually enjoyed. I was just creating one of those pieces rattling inside someone's alarm clock.

With a newfound interest in the intersection of business and technology, I made the leap from semiconductor engineer to semiconductor analyst. For you, this change probably sounds like I'm splitting hairs. For me, it was epic. Instead of building things, I would advise the people who built things. Somehow, I thought I could keep hiding in my head and simply write about technology. No one told me until I had the job that I would have to talk to people constantly; and not just one-on-one, but on stage and often in front of hundreds.

I don't know what I was more afraid of—speaking in public or resigning from a new job just days after being hired. As I paced the halls of my company hoping to find a way out of this mess, I noticed a sign on the wall that read "Toastmasters Public Speaking Club—Today at 12 pm in Room 1002." With a mixture of desperation and trepidation, I grabbed lunch from the cafeteria and headed to the conference room. My plan was to learn by watching. To guard against being called on to speak, I sat in the back corner with my eyes down, chewing away on my chicken sandwich. I felt like I was eight years old all over again.

Things went on like this every Wednesday for several weeks until two members of the club, Joshua Reynolds and Grant DuBois, urged me to give my first Table Topic. Table Topics are one- to two-minute impromptu speeches that answer a softball question like "If you could travel anywhere in the world, where would you go and why?" Joshua and Grant, both full-time editors of research reports, were men of words. They were not only skilled writers but also expert speakers. Joshua was a strapping six foot four and able to take on a variety of colorful stage personas from Baptist minister to Shakespearean actor. Grant, of more normal stature and slightly balding, was both passionate and cerebral. I longed to one day become half as good a speaker as they were.

I have no recollection of what I spoke about that day, but I do remember sweating, shaking, needing to control my bladder, not knowing what to do with my hands, and saying "um" after "um" after "um." And despite all that, people clapped for me. There is no pass or fail in a Toastmasters meeting. You win every time you get up on stage.

I came back to this safe environment week after week. I spoke occasionally and ultimately graduated to delivering longer prepared speeches, up to seven minutes. But most of the time, I watched and deconstructed how people structured and delivered their material.

After 10 years and 10,000 hours of effort under the guidance of great mentors, I reached the early stages of what Malcolm Gladwell would call an "outlier." Though my fear never went away (it never does), I learned how to transform my energy into passionate delivery. I became that passionate conversationalist that Joshua Reynolds and Grant DuBois had modeled for me such a long time ago.

Looking back, I am somewhat ashamed to admit that my first 10-year journey was a selfish one. It was mostly about how I could become a better speaker so that I could gain an edge in my personal and my professional life. Like too many speakers, I hoarded my knowledge in a thrice-sealed vault in my brain. And then, one day, something clicked.

I discovered that coaching other speakers was far more rewarding than focusing solely on my own ability to present. Though I wish I could say it happened in a single moment, the truth is that my epiphany was gradual. I began writing notes during every speech I watched, including a mix of supportive observations and constructive feedback. Rather than keep these to myself, I handed them discreetly to the speakers. Though I no doubt offended hordes of people by handing them unsolicited feedback lacking any identifying contact information, many of my friends and coworkers began to actively seek my advice. I had cemented my personal brand as a public speaking supernerd.

When you scream your passion, you attract opportunity. Six years after I started handing out speaker notes, I was having dinner with one of my closest friends, Neerav Shah. Neerav and I are brothers from another mother. We both married our college sweethearts and have two children around the same ages. We both left semi-conductor engineering for general management. And we are both voracious readers of business nonfiction. When he asked, "Have you heard of TED?" I figured that he was talking about some new bestselling author and responded, "Who's Ted?"

When I got home that night, I found an e-mail from Neerav with a link to Sir Ken Robinson's TED Talk.[1] I watched it, and watched it, and watched it again. I was hooked. TED Talks are caffeine for normal people; they are crystal meth for speaking nerds. TED Talks are more than entertaining; they are inspirational. Moreover, they are packed with ideas that not only are worth spreading but also are worth applying . . . immediately.

In the unlikely event that you have not yet watched one of the TED Talk videos, TED is a nonprofit organization devoted to amplifying electrifying ideas from the domains of *technology, entertainment,* and *design* (TED). Though TED has a variety of ventures, the two most notable are its highly exclusive conferences and its highly inclusive practice of posting presentations for free online.

If you are an avid viewer of TED videos, then you probably remember what it was like to watch your first TED video. Eighteen minutes of pure inspiration. TED's mission is to share ideas worth spreading, and its missionaries do not disappoint. Though not household names, Sir Ken Robinson, Jill Bolte Taylor, and a thousand others mesmerize their audiences with powerful content, delivery, and design.

TED Talks are a bit like an addiction in that they can consume you and affect the people you love. I realized this when my 12-year-old daughter started reciting passages verbatim from Ken Robinson's talk and when, after seeing Jill Bolte Taylor in freeze-frame on my laptop, she said, "Dad, that's the woman who talked about her stroke, right?" This is an addiction that I am glad I have passed on, since the prevalence of texting and social networks is creating a generation of people who will struggle to verbally express their ideas. Those who learn how to communicate offline will have a better chance of being heard and of making a difference in an ever-more crowded world.

Coming from an analytical background, I naturally developed a method for extracting the maximum value from TED Talks both as a normal viewer and as a speaking nerd. Though the talks are a maximum of 18 minutes, the process takes me a little over an hour per talk because I watch each video three times.

The first time I watch a TED Talk, my objective is to capture the essence of the speaker's idea and the narrative structure the speaker used to deliver it. Most speakers make it easy by explicitly stating their idea at either the beginning or the end. Others hide the idea just deep enough to give the listener the delight of experiencing the epiphany. Additionally, I strive to identify how the speakers opened their talk, how they built up the body, and how they concluded. Though the familiar "introduction, three parts, and a conclusion" structure is the most common, some speakers deviate from that pattern. When done intentionally, it is insightful to understand why it was done. During this first viewing, I also capture how the speaker used premises (declarative statements or propositions) and proof to build his case. Since so much proof is in the form of story, I extract creative ways to use plot, characters, and setting.

Whereas the first viewing gives me a macroperspective of the speaker's content, the second viewing allows me to narrow my focus on two specific elements. The first element is language. Because language includes humor, which is such a fundamental part of why TED Talks go viral, I built a little computer application that counts the position of each laugh when I click a button. If I have access to a transcript, then I count the use of words like *you, I,* and *we* as well as the number of questions the speaker asks in order to get a sense of the speaker's tone. Last, I seek out interesting turns of phrase that amplify the speaker's message.

The second element is delivery, both verbal and nonverbal. When I close my eyes and listen closely, I hear how the speakers use variation in volume, speed, and pitch. I also hear how they pause for different effects. Opening my eyes, I see how they communicated their emotions through facial expressions and body language.

The third and final viewing is dedicated to understanding design, including the use of slides, videos, and props. I count the number of slides using the same application that I use to count laughs. I try to understand my intellectual and emotional reaction to each speaker's use of images, text, and animation. Though video clips are fairly rare in TED Talks, the speakers who use them do apply certain best practices in how they select, edit, and present them. Props are similarly rare, and there are right ways and wrong ways to use them.

The pages that follow provide a how-to guide for delivering an inspiring speech based on intensive study of the most popular TED Talks. Commenting on an earlier version of this book, a reviewer wrote something along the lines of "You don't need to buy this book if you just watch the top 10 TED Talks and then watch the ones that aren't as popular to see the differences." That critic was correct! That said, my goal is to reveal the secrets and save you 20 years of studying public speaking and countless hours of watching and deconstructing hundreds of great and mediocre TED Talks.

In writing this book, I recognize that you may never actually deliver a TED Talk. However, you need to be able to express your ideas in a way that inspires others. That is true whether you are speaking to 1 person, 10 people, 100 people, or even 1,000 people. The same techniques that apply to a TED Talk apply to business presentations and meetings; no one ever said that boring your colleagues is the way to climb the corporate ladder. These techniques apply to all manner of public speaking, whether in schools or at conferences, as well as at weddings and other special occasions.

This book is divided into four parts that mirror your journey as a speaker from conception to delivery and beyond. In each part, I provide examples of how to apply best practices and avoid common pitfalls.

Part I focuses on content by covering how to choose ideas worth spreading, how to build and organize your talk, and how to tell stories. Though you tell stories every day, you may not have been exposed to techniques that will make your stories engaging for a large audience. This part also covers the finer aspects of storytelling, including structuring your plot, constructing your setting, and bringing colorful characters to life.

Part II explores the primary facets of verbal and nonverbal delivery. You will learn how to use your voice, your face, your body, and the stage to engage your audience.

Part III covers how to design slides that inspire and how to deliver video that captivates. As you will learn, I am not a huge fan of using slides or videos when speaking in public. However, there are times when words alone cannot do justice to your idea. In this part, I also touch on using props and using a lectern properly.

Part IV covers the journey to the stage and beyond. I address the more practical aspects of how one is selected to give a TED Talk, what you can do to manage your fear, and how you can help your videos gain traction.

The world has more than its share of armchair athletes, armchair travelers, and armchair critics. The last thing the world needs is armchair speakers. Reading about speaking will kick-start your growth. It may even give you greater confidence. But the only way to become a good, let alone great, speaker is to abide by the punch line to the old joke: "How do you get to Carnegie Hall?" The answer: "Practice! Practice! Practice!" As you digest portions of this book, find opportunities to practice in one-on-one conversations, in meetings, and at local Toastmasters clubs. And if the stars align just right, you might find yourself on the TED stage. I'll be the one cheering loudest for you from the audience and waiting to get my hands on your video to learn from and to share your magic.

PART I

CONTENT

CHAPTER 1

Choosing an Idea Worth Spreading

TIP 1: Everybody has an idea worth spreading.

After watching a TED Talk, most people feel at least two emotions. The first comes from the angel on your right shoulder whispering softly, "You can do anything. You can be anything. Go change the world." It makes you tingle with a sense of exhilaration about how your life and the lives of the people around you will change as you apply this newfound knowledge. The second emotion comes from the devil on your left shoulder who sows self-doubt by screaming, "You will never be able to give a talk like that! You don't even have a *good* idea, let alone a *great* idea. The only thing you have spent 10,000 hours over 10 years learning is how to watch television. You don't have a glamorous job. Nothing amazing has ever happened to you."

The first step in being able to deliver a TED Talk is telling the devil to go back to where he came from. He could not be more wrong. Just look at the evidence. For every Bill Gates, there are hundreds if not thousands of activists who have given talks about causes they have championed without the backing of a foundation with an endowment exceeding $30 billion. In fact, antipoverty activist Bunker Roy[1]—hardly a household name—delivered a TED Talk that has had nearly three times as many views as Mr. Gates's.[2] If you have transformed even one life for the better, including your own, then you have the seed of an idea worth spreading.

TIP 2: Choose your persona based on whether your primary objective is to educate, entertain, or inspire.

Before you say, "But, I'm not an activist," remember that speeches have been given by people from nearly every walk of life. Though TED started in 1984 with a focus on bringing together people from the worlds of technology, entertainment, and design, the organization has intentionally broadened its scope. In my sampling of TED Talks, I have identified no less than 15 common personas, falling into three categories, that frequently grace the stage.

These 15 personas are neither mutually exclusive nor collectively exhaustive. You may recognize yourself in more than one of them, or you may find yourself in none. Day to day and moment to moment, each of us changes hats. The point is simply that projecting these personas onto yourself one at a time will help you narrow your focus. Since constraints unlock creativity, this technique will help you easily identify which idea you want to spread. In addition, whether your dominant mission is education, entertainment, or inspiration, make sure to include a healthy dose of the other two components with information, humor, or emotion.

Category 1. The Educators

Though every great TED Talk is a mixture of education, entertainment, and inspiration, speakers in this category tend to have a heavier focus on the education component. By educator, I use a rather broad definition that is inclusive of those who seek to understand the nature of nature, the nature of people, and the nature of things people create. While not a requirement, these speakers often have advanced academic degrees in the sciences or engineering. The following four types of personas are in this category:

- *The inventor.* Inventors are the purveyors of cool. They share new technologies that promise to save us effort, entertain us, or even fulfill our dreams. From Pranav Mistry's SixthSense wearable electronics[3] to Sebastian Thrun's driverless car,[4] a large set of inventions discussed at TED focuses on the user experience with our gadgets. Ranking the most popular TED Talks by inventors reveals insights about our collective zeitgeist. One pattern that is telling—if not also a little funny—is that there is an unusually large concentration of TED Talks about things that fly, including robots, animals, and even people with jetpacks. The thirst for flight is more than a fad; it is a psychologically hardwired desire.

- *The life scientist.* Life scientists open our eyes to the wonders of living organisms, biological processes, and interrelationships among living things. As one might expect, the majority of the most viewed TED Talks by life scientists center on helping individuals understand their brains, stay healthy, and live longer. It appears that the same psychological survival instinct driving popularity for inventors is at play here. Three exceptional talks in this group include Jill Bolte Taylor's "Stroke of Insight,"[5] Hans Rosling's "Stats That Reshape Your Worldview,"[6] and Aubrey de Grey's "A Roadmap to End Aging."[7]

- *The natural scientist.* The laws of nature and the physical world—inclusive of astronomy, biology, chemistry, and physics—are made accessible to the masses by natural scientists. Through the words and images of these speakers, you can journey from subatomic particles (Brian Greene[8]), to underwater astonishments (David Gallo[9]), to the larger universe (Stephen Hawking[10]).

- *The social scientist.* Social scientists provide insights on the individual and collective human experience. Here, you will find two of the most popular TED Talks, Sir Ken Robinson's "Schools Kill Creativity"[11] and Brené Brown's "The Power of Vulnerability."[12] A large number of these talks help us make sense of our emotions such as love, empathy, and shame. The best of the presenters, like Dr. Brown, turn what we commonly perceive as negative into positive. Social scientists are the originators of the research commonly cited by another role you will read about in a few moments, the personal guru.

Category 2. The Entertainers

With the educators securely tucked away, we turn our attention to the next group, the entertainers. While their dominant mode is quite obviously to entertain, the best speakers in this category teach us by sharing the secrets of their craft.

- *The comedian.* Despite the organization's early commitment to entertainment, there are rather few TED Talks by comedians. Megastars like Jerry Seinfeld and Chris Rock rarely grace the TED stage. Sarah Silverman, a popular yet polarizing comedian, gave a rather explicit TED Talk in 2010 that is not available on YouTube or TED.com.[13] Ms. Silverman shares why: "It was never officially released because [TED curator] Chris Anderson called it 'god awful.'" Why so few comedians? The best comedy is pure entertainment. Professional comics need to deliver an astonishing four to six laughs per minute. To achieve a surprise every 10 seconds, they need to continually shift their direction, which makes it nearly impossible to construct an idea worth spreading. However, a few skilled performers managed to form a message out of the madness, including Charlie Todd,[14] Ze Frank,[15] Reggie Watts,[16] and Maz Jobrani.[17]

- *The magician.* TED audiences like to see performers deconstruct their craft. In the case of comedians, deconstructing the
  craft kills the humor. In the case of magicians, deconstructing
  the craft is a violation of the Magician's Oath, which prevents
  the sharing of the secrets behind illusions with nonmagi-
  cians. Though often a personal oath, it is also a foundation of
  the code of ethics in most professional magicians' societies.
  As a consequence of this limitation and of the requirement
  to have an idea worth spreading, one tends to find less traditional magicians on the TED stage. Examples include Arthur
  Benjamin ("Mathemagic"[18]), Keith Barry ("Brain Magic"[19]),
  and Marco Tempest ("Augmented Reality, Techno-Magic"[20]).
  Though not technically a magician, I put fraud debunker James
  Randi[21] in this category as well.

- *The writer.* The writer persona includes creators of fiction
  and poetry. Here is where you will find Elizabeth Gilbert,[22]
  Chimamanda Adichie,[23] and Isabel Allende[24] talking not only
  about their craft but also about their personal journeys as writers. My favorite in this category is Karen Thompson Walker,[25]
  who weaves a historical narrative with a counterintuitive message about what fear can teach us.

- *The performing artist.* This group includes dancers, musicians,
  and singers, as well as actors and directors of stage and screen.
  Though there are many traditional performances that are pure
  entertainment, the best talks by these types of artists mix
  performance with insight. For example, conductor Benjamin
  Zander[26] illustrated how "the job of the C [note] is to make the
  B [note] sad" in Chopin's "Prelude in E Minor." Though you
  never need to know why music makes you feel the way you do,
  it is enlightening to discover at least one reason why.

- *The visual artist.* Visual artists using nearly every medium
  are well represented in popular TED Talks. Candy Chang[27]

breathes new life into abandoned public spaces and structures. Erik Johansson[28] shares his incredible photography. You can also find the intersection of technology and art in many talks, including Beau Lotto's[29] optical illusions.

Category 3. Change Agents

Having covered technology and entertainment, you would expect the next group of TED personas to fall into the design category. However, design is more of a philosophy adopted by speakers of all kinds and transcends rigid classification. If technologists educate and entertainers entertain, then we need a third group to hold personas whose principal mission is to inspire. I call this largest of the three groups "change agents." If you did not find yourself in one of the prior categories, then you should adopt one of the following personas to share your idea worth spreading:

- *The activist.* Nearly every TED speaker is an activist in some way. So think of this role as someone vigorously engaged in driving social, political, or environmental change often by drawing attention to an immediate injustice. Three excellent speakers who conform to this persona include Bunker Roy, Jamie Oliver,[30] and Temple Grandin.[31]

- *The authority.* The authority persona is the most general. This category refers to speakers who share the epiphanies they experienced in their interesting, sometimes enviable, day jobs. The most popular talks in this category include Rory Sutherland's "Life Lessons from an Ad Man,"[32] Cameron Russell's "Looks Aren't Everything. Believe Me, I'm a Model,"[33] and Peter van Uhm's "Why I Chose a Gun."[34] Mr. Sutherland, a senior executive at a marketing firm, shares a counterintuitive idea about using psychological advertising techniques for good rather than for evil. Ms. Russell and Mr. van Uhm take similar approaches in challenging conventional wisdom about what it is like to be a fashion model and military commander, respectively.

- *The business guru.* Business gurus are the successful nonfiction authors and business authorities who curate and popularize esoteric social science to help others become more successful at work. Though there are exceptions such as Sheryl Sandberg,[35] this is a disproportionately male-dominated category that includes the likes of Simon Sinek,[36] Dan Pink,[37] and Seth Godin.[38]

- *The explorer.* Where authorities reveal epiphanies experienced in their day jobs, explorers share insights from personal experience. In some instances, they share stories about near-death experiences such as plane crashes (Ric Elias[39]) or brutal muggings (Ed Gavagan[40]). But it is just as effective to describe a positive practice that many dream of but never do; Matt Cutts's[41] "Try Something New for 30 Days" is a nice example of this. Ordinary-man Joe Smith[42] proved that even the mundane can be transformed into an idea worth spreading with his "How to Use a Paper Towel."

- *The personal guru.* Personal gurus are to the self-help section of the bookstore what business gurus are to the professional motivation section. And just as in the self-help section, you will find subsections devoted to love and sexuality, happiness, and religion. There are time-tested megastars here, including Tony Robbins,[43] Malcolm Gladwell,[44] and Mary Roach.[45] However, there are also plenty of newly minted phenoms such as introvert champion Susan Cain[46] and personal health guide Ron Gutman.[47] Most personal gurus, like their business counterparts, are writers.

- *The social entrepreneur.* There is a rather thin line between social entrepreneurs and activists, although in truth many speakers straddle both categories. The principal difference is

that social entrepreneurs apply business management principles to social change. This category includes free online
education advocate Salman Khan,[48] video game designer Jane
McGonigal,[49] and clean-water innovator Michael Pritchard.[50]

TIP 3: Frame your idea worth spreading as an action-outcome response to a question worth asking.

Excluding TED Talks whose sole purpose is to entertain, the main
mission of most TED Talks is to call listeners to action in such a way
that makes the world a better place. Many of the most satisfying
talks recommend that listeners take tiny actions that can lead to
large personal and societal benefits. Since people are naturally stuck
in their ways, the tiny actions suggested need to be fast, cheap, and
easy. One of my favorite examples is Joe Smith, who started his talk
at TEDxConcordiaUPortald in 2012 with the following:

> *If we [Americans] could reduce the usage of paper towels, one
> paper towel per person per day, 571,230,000 pounds of paper
> [would] not [be] used.*

While there is no single best way to phrase your idea worth
spreading during your talk, there is an excellent way to think about
it during the planning stages. To impose good discipline, the format
I recommend is "To (action) so that (outcome)." Let's look at the
questions that trigger ideas worth spreading and how individual
speakers answered them, starting with the technologists:

- *The inventor.* MIT Media Labs wizard Pranav Mistry asked
  himself, "How do I accelerate the development and adoption
  of technology that will close the digital divide and restore our
  connection to the physical world?" He answered with this
  idea worth spreading: "To promote the development of digital

gadgets that people can interact with using natural gestures so that we do not end up as machines sitting in front of other machines."

- *The life scientist.* Neuroscientist Jill Bolte Taylor asked herself, "How can I combine my personal experience and my scientific knowledge to give people a way to treat each other more compassionately?" She answered with the idea worth spreading, "To choose to live in the collective consciousness of your brain's right hemisphere (rather than the self-centric left hemisphere) so that we can have a more peaceful world."

- *The natural scientist.* Mycologist Paul Stamets[51] asked himself, "How can I alert people to an unobserved but growing threat to the survival of all living organisms?" He answered with the idea worth spreading, "To preserve the biodiversity of mushrooms in old-growth forests so that we prevent the mass extinction of life on earth."

- *The social scientist.* Sir Ken Robinson asked, "What small change can we make to our education system that will unleash the hidden potential of our collective but repressed creativity?" He answered with the idea worth spreading, "To educate the whole being of children, their right and left brain, so that they can build a brighter future."

Now, let's turn our attention to the entertainers:

- *The comedian.* Improv Everywhere founder Charlie Todd asked himself, "How can I get adults to recapture the uninhibited bliss of their childhoods?" He answered with the idea worth spreading, "To accept that there is no right or wrong way to play so that we can have more joy."

- *The magician.* Mathemagician Arthur Benjamin asked himself, "How do I convince people that normal minds can perform impossible tasks?" He answered with the idea worth spreading, "To use clever shortcuts so that complex problems become easy." If you listen to his talk, it is hard to catch this since he never states it explicitly. However, he illustrates it when he reveals that the trick to squaring large numbers is to break them down into the sum of three simpler calculations. For example, what is 68 squared? You could calculate it as 68 times 68, which is mind blowing for most people. Or you could sum 60 times 60 (3,600) plus 8 times 8 (64) plus 60 times 8 times 2 (960). Either way, the answer is 4,624. Maybe that is not easy, but it is at least easier.

- *The writer.* Fiction writer Chimamanda Adichie asked herself, "How do I prevent people from making the mistakes I made about my own identity and about my perception of the identities of others?" She answered with the idea worth spreading, "To reject stereotypes as incomplete stories so that we embrace the true diversity of individuals and groups."

- *The performing artist.* Conductor Benjamin Zander asked himself, "How can I ignite people's passion for an underappreciated form of art?" He answered with the idea worth spreading, "To embrace classical music so that you can experience deep emotion."

- *The visual artist.* Urban artist Candy Chang asked herself, "How do I help people experience emotional catharsis?" She answered with the idea worth spreading, "To repurpose abandoned public spaces as anonymous message boards so that people can express their deepest secrets and dreams."

Finally, consider the questions and answers of the change agents:

- *The activist.* Indian activist Bunker Roy asked himself, "How can I empower the disenfranchised to empower themselves?" He answered with the idea worth spreading, "To empower rural women with knowledge so that they can improve the standard of living in their communities."

- *The authority.* Advertising executive Rory Sutherland asked himself, "How can I challenge people's conventional wisdom about my profession?" He answered with the idea worth spreading, "To encourage people to embrace intangible value so that we increase our perceived wealth and conserve limited resources."

- *The business guru.* Author and thinker Simon Sinek asked himself, "What is the fastest way to improve the success of individuals and corporations?" He answered with the idea worth spreading, "To encourage leaders to start with why so that they can inspire others."

- *The explorer.* Though he is a search algorithm engineer at Google, the persona Matt Cutts adopted for his TED Talk had nothing to do with his day job. He was just an ordinary person trying to improve his life. He asked himself, "What one tip can I share from my self-improvement journey that inspires and teaches others how to improve their lives?" He answered with the idea worth spreading, "To stick to a new habit (or remove a bad one) for 30 days so that you can achieve lasting positive change."

- *The personal guru.* Self-help author Susan Cain asked herself, "How can I help people accept themselves and others for who they are?" She answered with the idea worth spreading, "To show introverts that they contribute equal value to the world as extroverts, though often in different ways, so that introverts do not feel the need to change what gives them creativity and energy."

- *The social entrepreneur.* Former hedge fund analyst turned online educator Salman Khan asked himself, "How do I help my cousins living 1,500 miles away do better in school?" From that humble beginning came a gigantic idea worth spreading: "To build an online, global classroom so that everyone can increase their math and science aptitude."

Selecting a topic requires an act of deep introspection beginning with the end in mind. There is a good chance that one of the questions I've listed will trigger a great topic for your speech. If that does not work, you can further generalize by asking questions of self-discovery such as the following: "What is the greatest lesson I ever learned?" "What is the greatest joy I ever experienced?" "The greatest misery?" "What is my life's mission, and how can I enlist others to join my crusade?"

If all else fails, then you can ask, "What is the most amazing story I can tell?" Though stories are the centerpiece of most TED Talks, they are the proof for the point that you want to make. Hence, if you begin your topic discovery with a story, you need to focus on making sure that the moral is clear.

TIP 4: Sow a single seed of inspiration.

After each audience member leaves the auditorium or surfs on to the next website, you should have planted one idea that either awakens the person's consciousness to a new way of thinking or persuades him or her to take action. This will achieve your objective to sow a single seed of inspiration.

Most of the time, the best way to approach topic selection is to pick a single unifying message that you want to deliver and then scour your brain for amazing experiences that add emotional depth to the logical argument of your message. If you get stuck, do it the other way around. No one will ever know. What is key here, and I cannot stress this enough, is to have a crystal-clear understanding of your central idea before you do anything else. One of the biggest mistakes speakers make is trying to pack a lifetime of learning in a single talk. A laser focus on a single concept gives you the clarity to edit your material. If you have a great concept or story that does not directly support your message, then you have to omit it, no matter how much you want to use it.

Not infrequently, speakers deliver an artfully crafted, highly focused talk until they reach their conclusion. In what in their minds is a great act of compassion, they bolt on one or more additional pieces of advice worth spreading. This often comes in the form of a story with a different moral than the one central to their talk. Unfortunately, this jumble of ideas severely limits the overall impact of the speech.

There are, of course, many TED Talks that never get posted on TED.com. Often, the reason is that speakers lacked focus throughout the course of their speech and failed to sow a single seed of inspiration.

TIP 5: Connect with people's deep-rooted needs for belonging, self-interest, self-actualization, or hope for the future.

Of the 10 most viewed TED Talks, 7 focused on inspiring people to change themselves. There is no novelty in the concepts they address; there is nothing new under the sun. (Case in point—that expression is a 2,000-year-old biblical quote from Ecclesiastes.) Those seven talks focused on concepts inside the human mind, including mental illness, creativity, leadership, happiness, motivation, success, and self-worth.

The other three most viewed TED Talks cast a wider net by catalyzing interpersonal and societal change. They called us to action or altered our perspective on public health, public education, and diversity. The speakers who gave these talks were not the first to explore those subjects, and they will not be the last. They touched us by giving their perspective on why these ideas matter and how you can make a difference.

As you think about making emotional connections that inspire your audience, keep in mind that people generally have four fundamental needs that emerge after meeting our basic needs for physiological health and physical security.

The first of the four is the need for love and belonging. In mid-2011, Gerda Grimshaw posted the question "What makes you happy?" on the TED discussion group on LinkedIn. Gerda is founder of Call Mom, a free referral service that connects single mothers and their children with resources and education to help them become self-sufficient and to thrive. Of the more than 100 responses generated, 92 of them were people genuinely sharing the source of their happiness. Though my approach was not unimpeachably scientific, I classified and categorized the responses to understand the secret behind contentment. As you can see from the following, love and belonging, expressed via social interaction, dominates the list:

- Social interaction with family, friends, and, yes, pets (30.4 percent)

- Experiencing nature (12.0 percent)

- Charity and volunteering (10.9 percent)

- Task completion (9.8 percent)

- Inspiring others though coaching, teaching, or writing (7.6 percent)

- Introspection and learning (7.6 percent)

- Mindfulness or "being in the moment" (6.5 percent)

- Good health—particularly among people with recent or chronic illness (5.4 percent)

- Physical pleasure and exercise (5.4 percent)

- Self-expression (2.2 percent)

- Financial well-being (2.2 percent)

The second of the fundamental deep-rooted needs is desire and self-interest. In the above list, physical pleasure, exercise, and financial well-being all fall into this group. Truth be told, the frequency of these items in the general population is probably a bit higher, but it is socially taboo to comment on these desires in LinkedIn's mostly squeaky clean and not anonymous discussion groups. Lest you think such subjects are not the stuff of TED Talks, think again. Mary Roach shared "10 Things You Did Not Know About Orgasm" in her TED2009 presentation, and Helen Fisher[52] revealed "Why We Love + Cheat" in her TED2006 performance. There are plenty of talks on money too, albeit with a slant toward inspiring people to overcome their inhibitions and pursue their entrepreneurial dreams.

Accelerating personal development is the third fundamental need that you can access to connect with your audience. We all want to learn and to grow. We are curious about ourselves, and we work to challenge and ultimately overcome our limitations. We are equally curious about the world around us. By way of example, if you have a recipe for setting and achieving goals, then you have the makings of a great TED Talk. The mechanics of this kind of topic are often used; what is novel is the story of how you have failed, learned, and overcome adversity.

It is no accident that "hope and change" was the centerpiece of Barack Obama's winning 2008 presidential campaign. It is the centerpiece of every mass movement, be it social, political, or religious. And it is the fourth of the fundamental needs that we have as human beings. To captivate your listeners, help them make an enemy of the status quo and see the positive promise of tomorrow that is just out of reach and worth the effort. At some point in our lives, we all wake up and stand before the insatiable chasm of existential meaninglessness. People need to make a difference. Give them the means and the will to make their dent in the universe.

TIP 6: Speak about a topic you are passionate about.

From this book you will absorb a Swiss Army knife's worth of techniques and tricks for delivering a powerful speech. As with any sharp object, please exercise caution. The single greatest danger in public speaking is losing authenticity by overengineering your talk. However, amazing things happen when you confine your speaking to a topic that you are passionate about. Your nerves subside. You automatically build persuasive arguments. Stories roll off your tongue. And your delivery becomes an afterthought. TED star Simon Sinek confirmed as much when I asked him how he delivered his magical talk:

> When people ask me how I learned to speak I tell them, truthfully, that I cheat! I only talk about things I care about and about things I understand. I can't manufacture passion. People who have kids can talk for hours about their kids. They tell story after story after story with such excitement. I do the same. The ideas I share are like children—I really, really care about them and I am excited to share stories about them to anyone who will listen.

Many people who write and speak about speaking advise you to figure out what the audience wants and then adapt your message to suit people's needs. This well-intentioned advice has a downside. While it is important to tailor content to an audience's needs, your alterations should be confined to cosmetic changes. For example, you might swap one vignette for another that your audience can more directly relate to. Or you might change the amount of background information you provide given your audience's prior knowledge. I believe it is far better to seek out audiences who want and need your ideas rather than bending like a reed in the wind. Fortunately TED audiences are eager to experience any idea worth spreading that educates, entertains, and inspires them.

TIP 7: Remember that you speak in service of your audience.

Having organized several TEDx events and been an advisor to organizers of many others, I am frequently approached by hopeful as well as established professional speakers for advice on how to get accepted to give a talk. Since I suspect most of you are more interested in improving your public speaking ability than in actually being on the TED stage, I will save a detailed overview of that topic for Part IV of this book. However, I would like to share with you the single most important piece of advice I share with them.

I respond to their question of how to get accepted for a talk with the question, "Why do you want to give a talk?" In most instances the response is, "Because this is a golden opportunity to build my brand," or "Because I have dreamed of giving a TED Talk ever since I saw my first TED video." You have to at least give them credit for their honesty.

The problem with these answers is that they are speaker centric rather than audience centric. TED organizers can smell this from a mile away, and it is a major turnoff. The right answer is, "Because I have an insatiable need to share an idea worth spreading even if it touches the heart and mind of just one person in the audience." With that answer, you have succeeded even if your video has quality problems and never makes it online.

I'll leave you with the advice that Simon Sinek gave me:

Most importantly, I always show up to give. I very often say it out loud to myself before I take the stage, "You're here to share your ideas today." Whenever I speak, I don't show up wanting anything from anyone—e.g., more business, approval, sell books, more

Twitter followers, or Facebook likes. I always show up to share what I know. If they like it then they will applaud, which is the best way for me gauge if what I gave was important to them.

Once you identify your idea worth spreading, you need to structure it in a way that makes it easy for your audience to absorb. The next chapter shows you how to organize your talk so that it touches your audience intellectually and emotionally.

CHAPTER 2

Organizing Your Talk

TIP 8: Determine whether you will deliver a story-driven or premise-driven narrative.

When constructing a talk, speakers develop either a story-driven narrative or a premise-driven narrative. Story-driven narratives typically focus on a single story from beginning to end. Most of the time the speaker is on stage, she actively relives her story. As a result, her logical argument will generally be implied until the very end when she reflects on her story and reveals the moral. This contrasts with a premise-driven narrative where the elements of the speaker's argument are well exposed throughout the talk. Though TED has a reputation for great storytelling, the fact is that most speakers deliver premise-driven narratives. TED Talks with premise-driven narratives often include multiple-story vignettes that play a supporting rather than lead role.

Usually, speakers who opt for a story-driven narrative recount their experiences in the first person. The most famous example in this category is Jill Bolte Taylor's "Stroke of Insight" TED talk.[1] Though I will cover story development in much greater depth in the next chapter, consider Ms. Taylor's story boiled down to its raw essence.

Jill's story begins with what she does and why she does it. We learn that she is a researcher studying severe mental illness at the Harvard Medical School Department of Psychiatry. She chose this life path in order to help individuals diagnosed with schizophrenia, including her brother. On December 10, 1996, when she was 37 years old, she woke up to discover that she was experiencing a rare type of stroke caused by bleeding that affected the language centers in the left hemisphere of her brain. As she struggled to figure out what was happening and how to get help, she experienced the euphoria of what it is like to shed the individual reality of her left brain and to live in the pure collective consciousness of the right brain. Fortunately, she managed to use her fleeting left-brain cognitive moments enough times to place a phone call to a colleague, who sent an ambulance. After undergoing surgery three weeks later to remove a golf-ball-size blood clot, she spent the next eight years making a gradual but ultimately full recovery. She ends her story in dramatic fashion with her moral:

> *I believe that the more time we spend choosing to run the deep inner-peace circuitry of our right hemispheres, the more peace we will project into the world, and the more peaceful our planet will be. And I thought that was an idea worth spreading.*

Perhaps a more apt description is to say that story-driven narratives are really story dominated because speakers do occasionally step out of the story to interpret what is happening or to follow important tangents. For example, Ms. Taylor departed from her story-driven narrative one time early in her speech for a necessary clinical explanation of the functioning of the sensory right hemisphere of the brain and the analytical left hemisphere. Until the end, that was the only time that she was not actively reliving her story.

TIP 9: Formulate the logical argument that proves your idea worth spreading.

If your central idea forms the spine of your talk, then your logical argument forms the ribs. This is true whether you build your talk using a story-driven or premise-driven narrative. Since story-driven narratives are heavy on moral but light on premise, the best way to understand the construction of logical arguments is to deconstruct the TED Talks that have premise-driven narratives. In order to do that, you need to understand the use of logic in public speaking.

No discussion of logic is complete without a refresher course in the difference between inductive and deductive reasoning. By its strictest definition, inductive reasoning proves a general principle—your idea worth spreading—by highlighting a group of specific events, trends, or observations. In contrast, deductive reasoning builds up to a specific principle—again, your idea worth spreading—through a chain of increasingly narrow statements.

Though I touch on these two ways to make an argument, please bear in mind that in their literal academic form both are very difficult to apply to speech construction. Even after watching hundreds of great TED Talks, I often struggle to pick apart the speaker's logical construction; not because it is absent or poorly framed, but because it is as subtle as it should be. Despite these challenges, understanding inductive and deductive reasoning is the key to great speechwriting.

With inductive reasoning, the general principle concluded is supported by the evidence but not with absolute certainly, because it is usually not feasible to observe every possible case. For example, imagine that you work in an animal shelter. Every day, your job is to shampoo the dogs that are brought to the shelter to remove their fleas. Since every dog that comes in has fleas, you conclude that all dogs have fleas. Now, that is a reasonable conclusion, especially given the compelling evidence you have. But if one day you encounter a flealess dog, then your conclusion would be disproved. Even the conclusion that most dogs have fleas has the same vulnerability since you may simply be observing only a particular subset of itchy canines.

Even though inductive reasoning is considered a bottoms-up approach, the general principle can be revealed at either the beginning or the end. Using the same example, admittedly not an idea worth spreading, you can say either of the following: (1) I have observed hundreds of dogs. Every one of them had fleas. Therefore, all dogs have fleas; or (2) All dogs have fleas. I know because I have observed hundreds of dogs. Every one of them had fleas.

Should you choose to reveal your key inductive insight at the beginning or at the end? It turns out there is a trade-off. When you reveal your general principle at the beginning, your listeners are able to easily follow along. They are less likely to wonder, "Where is he going with this?" Though people like drama, they can only handle so much of it. By taking the drama out of the logical argument, you can spend your "drama budget" elsewhere in your speech. In addition, the early reveal is most effective when your idea is one that most reasonable minds would readily accept. Of course, there are times when you want to build the drama and should disclose your crucial insight at the end. There is no perfect way, though I recommend sharing the idea worth spreading at the beginning for full-length (18-minute) talks since that is a long time to wait for the big reveal.

To apply inductive reasoning to public speaking, we need to keep the best bits, relax a few constraints, and thereby transform it into something useful. I call this something useful "premise groups."

Just as inductive reasoning starts or ends with a general principle, so too do premise groups. No differences yet.

Where inductive reasoning is built by assembling collections of events, trends, or observations, a premise group is constructed by chaining increasingly provocative statements. Every provocative statement triggers a question. For your logic to flow smoothly, your job is to plant and then immediately answer your audience's next most pressing question. If your statement is extremely provocative, then you will need to start by answering "why?" with reasons, observations, or causes. If the statement is more readily acceptable, then you need to address "how?" in steps or methods. Depending on the statement, you may trigger who, what, where, when, or some other question. Regardless of the question raised, notice that the set of answers is strictly described by a plural noun such as *reasons* or *steps*. The answers can be ordered by flow, such as process or chronological steps, or by priority from high to low.

By way of example, consider the talk Charlie Todd delivered at TEDxBloomington in 2011.[2] Mr. Todd is the founder of Improv Everywhere, a New York City–based prank collective that causes scenes of chaos and joy in public places. Stated another way, Mr. Todd and company institutionalized the concept of the nonviolent "flash mob" two years before that term was even coined.

Mr. Todd's TED Talk was highly entertaining, short at just over 11 minutes, and conveyed a noncontentious idea worth spreading. Hence, he was able to get away with holding his reveal—"to accept that there is no right or wrong way to play so that we can have more joy"—until the end of his talk. Charlie starts off his talk with a prologue explaining that he formed Improv Everywhere when he moved to New York City and did not have a stage available for acting and comedy. That opening triggers the question "How do you create an outdoor improvisational stage?" Illustrating his talk with video and photographs documenting his missions, he answers with five methods:

1. By causing a scene in a public place that is a positive experience for others and that gives them a great story to tell
2. By choosing locations that naturally attract an audience
3. By taking advantage of assets already in the environment
4. By making the project site-specific
5. By occasionally choosing to use leisure time in an unusual way

TIP 10: Touch your audiences' hearts and minds with premise and proof.

At some point during your formal education, you were probably taught that effective communications are structured using five elements: an introduction, three parts for the body, and a conclusion. You may also have been instructed to include the three Aristotelian modes of persuasion—ethos (speaker credibility), pathos (emotion), and logos (logic)—in your speeches. I agree wholeheartedly with this guidance; it is a great jumping-off point for structuring an inspiring speech. However, if you stop at just this level of knowledge, then you are likely to deliver a boring speech.

Imagine this in the hands of two types of speakers—one, a purely emotional storyteller, and the other, a purely logical educator. The purely emotional storyteller might entertain you brilliantly as he brings you through a range of emotions. Even if there is a compelling moral to the story, you will have to do a lot of work as a listener to extract the why, the how, and the what of his idea. In many cases, you will not be able to piece it together, and the gaps will prevent you from being inspired.

Conversely, consider what happens when you listen to a purely logical educator. Until I discovered TED, I was guilty of being this kind of speaker. I could provide rational justification for the particular argument or business case I was making. And yet I was struggling to persuade people because I failed to provide the proof that allowed my audiences to emotionally buy into what I was saying.

The breakthrough I had when watching TED videos is that the most compelling speakers blend premise and proof. These ingredients need not be mixed in exact proportions. As a rule of thumb, the more complex the argument, the more premises you need. Extending the body metaphor, the idea worth spreading is the spine, the premises are the ribs, and the proof is the flesh. You need all three in order for your speech to stand on its own.

TABLE 2.1

Five-Element Speech Outline with Premise and Proof

ELEMENT	PREMISE	PROOF
Introduction	Step 1	
Part A	Step 3	Step 2
Part B	Step 5	Step 4
Part C	Step 7	Step 6
Conclusion	Step 8	

Table 2.1 provides a TED Talk–ready outline that builds on the familiar five-element structure layering in premise and proof. In the outline, the speaker begins with the introduction (step 1) and then segues into Part A of the speech. Since people generally need emotion before reason, Part A starts with proof (step 2) followed by premise (step 3). The premise is the rational insight, explanation, or proposition gleaned from the proof point. The speaker then repeats this pattern in Part B and Part C while alternating between proof and premise in steps 4 through 7. Finally, the speaker ends with the conclusion (step 8).

Just like the basic five-element structure, this enhanced outline is meant to be a starting point rather than a rigid form. Some speakers leave out one or more of the eight steps. Other speakers prefer to state their premise first and then support it with proof. Plenty adjust the number of parts in the speech body. The variations are nearly limitless.

This has all been pretty abstract so far, and I imagine that you are dying for an actual example. The discussion has been all premises and no proof! So let's see how Charlie Todd adapted and applied this outline in his speech. As you can see in Table 2.2, Mr. Todd adapted the basic outline by having five rather than three major parts in the body of his speech.

TABLE 2.2

Outline of Charlie Todd's "The Shared Experience of Absurdity" TED Talk

ELEMENT	PREMISE	PROOF
Introduction	(1) Started Improv Everywhere 10 years ago when I moved to NYC but did not have a stage for acting and comedy	
Part A	(3) By causing a scene in a public place that is a positive experience for others that gives them a great story to tell	(2) "No Pants Subway Ride" video clip[*]
Part B	(5) By choosing locations that naturally attract an audience	(4) "Look Up More" video clip[†]
Part C	(7) By taking advantage of assets already in the environment	(6) "Best Buy Prank" video clip[‡]
Part D	(9) By making the project site-specific	(8) "High Five Escalator" video clip[§]
Part E	(11) By occasionally choosing to use leisure time in an unusual way	(10) Six examples supported by slides
Conclusion	(12) As children, we do not question play. As adults we must relearn that there is no right or wrong way to play.	

[*] Todd, Charlie. "No pants subway ride (2002)." ImprovEverywhere. <http://www.youtube.com/watch?v=217mhbpADN0>.
[†] Todd, Charlie. "Look up more." ImprovEverywhere. <http://www.youtube.com/watch?v=RSBXS1npqNI>.
[‡] Todd, Charlie. "Best Buy uniform prank." ImprovEverywhere. <http://www.youtube.com/watch?v=KgUIbPfhSuo>.
[§] Todd, Charlie. "High five escalator." ImprovEverywhere. <http://www.youtube.com/watch?v=Abt8aAB-Dr0>.

In Part A, he proves his first "how" by showing and narrating a video of an absurd prank on a female New York City subway rider and her fellow passengers. The story vignette evolves as follows. A woman is reading a book on a subway car. Two men are sitting across from her having a conversation. As the subway pulls into its first stop, the woman looks up and notices a man who just boarded wearing a coat and scarf but sporting only yellow polka-dot boxer shorts from the waist down. Six more men at six additional subway stops enter the train car the same way without communicating with each other. Ultimately, a woman boards the train holding a duffel bag and offers pants for sale for $1. The men put on their pants, leave the train, and go off in different directions.

TIP 11: Do not cram too much into your talk.

The greatest risk a speaker faces in building a TED Talk is having too much content. When you edit your talk, the first question to ask yourself is whether a given part of your speech either adds to your premises or adds to your proof. In the case of Charlie Todd's TED Talk, all five parts of the body of his speech pass this screen. The next question is whether you absolutely, positively need each part, especially when the number of parts exceeds the magical number three.

In general, it is a good idea to keep the type of proof that you are using consistent. Each of the first four parts of Charlie Todd's speech was nicely parallel in structure. Each part had a "how" supported by a video example that Mr. Todd narrated. However, his fifth part contained a blur of six examples supported by slides rather than videos. Since the treatment was so different, this part of the speech felt tacked on and rushed. It was as if Mr. Todd was cramming in the portfolio of his life's work. The work is brilliant, but the fifth part, Part E in Table 2.2, took away from the power of his talk. He could have dropped the extra examples and moved the leisure-time premise either up into his introduction or down into his conclusion.

TIP 12: Use proof that triggers an emotional response.

There is a common misconception that stories such as those Mr. Todd told are the only way to speak to the right brain. While I do feel that stories are the best form, proof can be delivered in many other forms including but not limited to statistics, quotes, examples, and even hypothetical situations. Let us look at each of these nonstory forms in turn starting with statistics.

The website 43Things.com has over 3 million subscribers who list their goals, share their progress, and cheer one another on. One of the most interesting things about the website is a summary of people's most popular goals, called the 43 Things Zeitgeist. The goal to "write a book" is near the top of the list, with similar aspirations such as "lose weight," "fall in love," and "save money." With that broadly relevant context, consider how TED2011 speaker Matt Cutts[3] broke down the statistics of what it really takes to write a book:

> I also figured out that if you really want something badly enough,
> you can do anything for 30 days. Have you ever wanted to write
> a novel? Every November, tens of thousands of people try to write
> their own 50,000-word novel from scratch in 30 days. It turns out,
> all you have to do is write 1,667 words a day for a month. So I did.
> By the way, the secret is not to go to sleep until you've written your
> words for the day. You might be sleep-deprived, but you'll finish
> your novel. Now is my book the next great American novel? No.
> I wrote it in a month. It's awful.

Quotations are a second form of nonstory proof commonly used during speeches. Since quotes have been overused to the point of becoming clichéd, I only advocate using them when the person you are quoting is either the subject of your speech or a significant character. Early in his TED Talk, social activist Bunker Roy[4] established Mahatma Gandhi as a significant albeit invisible influence, a mentor character, in Roy's efforts to build a college for the rural poor where they could share valuable, traditional knowledge:

> And we thought that these people should come into the main-
> stream and show that the knowledge and skills that they have is

universal. It needs to be used, needs to be applied, needs to be shown to the world outside—that these knowledge and skills are relevant even today. So the college works following the lifestyle and work-style of Mahatma Gandhi. You eat on the floor, you sleep on the floor, you work on the floor. There are no contracts . . .

With Gandhi tactfully established as a significant character in his speech, Mr. Roy concluded his talk with a quote that sums up his message empowering the repressed rural poor:

I'll end with a quotation by Mahatma Gandhi. "First they ignore you, then they laugh at you, then they fight you, and then you win."

Whether familiar or esoteric, examples are perhaps the most common form of nonstory proof in TED Talks and other speeches. Here, self-help guru Susan Cain[5] cites three individuals as examples, including the ever-present Gandhi, immediately after stating her premise:

Now in fact, some of our transformative leaders in history have been introverts. I'll give you some examples. Eleanor Roosevelt, Rosa Parks, Gandhi—all these people described themselves as quiet and soft-spoken and even shy. And they all took the spotlight, even though every bone in their bodies was telling them not to. And this turns out to have a special power all its own, because people could feel that these leaders were at the helm, not because they enjoyed directing others and not out of the pleasure of being looked at; they were there because they had no choice, because they were driven to do what they thought was right.

Hypothetical situations are one of the more elegant forms of nonstory proof because they stimulate listeners to convince themselves. Since this form of proof is so powerful, you often find it used in the opening or the conclusion of a talk. The speaker may ask the members of the audience to first imagine a dark world in which their advice is not heeded, and then the speaker releases the tension by having them imagine a brighter world in which their idea has taken hold. Or as Salman Khan[6] did in the conclusion to his talk, the speaker may focus only on the benefits. Kahn's premise is that technology-enabled, self-directed learning can lift humanity to a higher level of knowledge. Here is his proof:

> And as valuable as [self-directed learning] is in Los Altos, imagine what that does to the adult learner who's embarrassed to go back and learn stuff that they should have before, before going back to college. Imagine what it does to a street kid in Calcutta who has to help his family during the day, and that's the reason why he or she can't go to school. Now they can spend two hours a day and remediate, or get up to speed and not feel embarrassed about what they do or don't know.

TIP 13: Use premise chains for the radical or nuanced ideas worth spreading.

Thus far, we have taken an in-depth look at one type of narrative—the inductive premise group. That structure is actually the most common form used in TED Talks, since most ideas worth spreading are not terribly counterintuitive. Many speakers play the role of professional reminder by prompting us to do the things we know we should do or think the way we know we should think. These speakers not only put the idea back under your nose but also spin a good yarn and provide some nice tricks and tips to build new habits.

Sometimes the speaker has an idea worth spreading that strongly defies conventional wisdom. In that case, inductive premise groups will not work because they are based on a process that leaves room for doubt. (Remember, if you come across one dog without fleas, then your whole "all dogs have fleas" general principle is shot.)

Fortunately, there is another narrative structure using deductive reasoning that will do the trick.

Going back to the strict textbook definition, deductive logic begins with the statement of a generally accepted principle, rule, or law that is noncontroversial. It must be noncontroversial since you need to ease people into your argument; if they challenge the first thing you say, then they are going to fight you all the way through. With the first principle established, deductive reasoning then chains together increasingly specific yet equally accepted premises. For this reason, this type of reasoning is considered top-down. In the end, the speaker reaches an often surprising conclusion—an idea worth spreading. Since it is based on a series of truths, the idea has the power of being proved with absolute certainty.

Since I cannot seem to resist dog examples, here is another: (1) All dogs have fleas. (2) All fleas bite. (3) Flea bites are itchy. (4) Animals lacking impulse control scratch every itch. (5) Dogs are animals lacking impulse control. (6) Therefore, all dogs scratch themselves. Yes, it is a little silly and certainly not an idea worth spreading, but it helps convey the point. At minimum it is a three-step process with one major premise, one minor premise, and one conclusion that links them together. The chain can be infinite. Also note that whereas inductive reasoning can develop with the big insight either at the beginning or at the end, deductive reasoning always reveals the idea worth spreading at the end.

Like its inductive sibling, unmodified deductive reasoning is too rigid to apply to public speaking. The key to transforming it for use in TED Talks is to recognize that each step in a deductive argument is a link in a linear chain. Each link raises a question that is answered by the next link in the "premise chain."

The most beautifully constructed premise chains are chains of "whys." If you have ever had a conversation with a six-year-old, you have seen this in action. Adults dread the fourth or fifth why because it gets really hard to answer after that point; and responding with an infuriated "Because!" does not win you any awards as a parent.

When you are able to answer why in progressive depth, you will get to a very elegant solution.

You can also have chains of all other kinds, including chains of hows, chains of whats . . . chains of just about anything. Moreover, you can answer different questions, proceeding, for example, from why to how to what. The critical, and I mean critical, requirement is that each link in the chain answers the most pressing question raised by the prior link. If you fail to do that, your argument will crumble.

In a speech with an introduction, three parts in the body, and a conclusion, you can deliver a major premise, three minor premises, and a powerful ending insight. This is precisely what Sir Ken Robinson[7] did in his talk, as shown in Table 2.3.

Rather than state his big idea up front, Sir Ken built up to it progressively using the situation-complication-resolution framework. (Many people call this the problem-solution format, but I prefer to break it into three pieces since listeners need context before they can appreciate the problem raised by the complication.) The situation-complication-resolution structure offers the most efficient way to lead people on a three-part journey that changes their perspective or calls them to action. In the first part, you describe the situation at hand in a fairly neutral manner. A good way to do this is to imagine that you are providing background context to a person who is intelligent and interested but does not have significant prior knowledge. In the second part, the complication section, you hook the audience by revealing why the current state of the world is flawed. Flaws may not only be problems but also be hidden opportunities. In the final part, offer a solution that neatly and completely resolves the problems or harnesses the opportunities you cited earlier.

Sir Ken begins his premise chain with the first noncontroversial statement he can make about the subject of creativity in education. Starting with something that any reasonable listener would agree with is a proven best practice in the art of persuasion. Every statement generates a multitude of potential questions. As I mentioned previously, the speaker's job is to address the most pressing question

TABLE 2.3

Outline of Sir Ken Robinson's "Do Schools Kill Creativity?" TED Talk

ELEMENT	PREMISE	PROOF
Introduction	(1) Creativity in education is as important as literacy	
Part A	(3) Children are inherently creative	(2) Share stories about: (a) A six-year-old girl who drew a picture of G-d (b) His son playing Joseph in a nativity play
Part B	(5) However, we are educating children out of their creative capacity to meet the needs of our industrialized society. Rather than creating a better world, we are simply fueling academic inflation	(4) Package up a mix of: (a) A quote by Picasso (b) A story about moving to America (c) A statistic from UNESCO
Part C	(7) Instead, we should embrace the diversity of human intelligence	(6) Tell a story about Gillian Lynne, who developed a successful career as a dancer and choreographer
Conclusion	(8) Therefore, we must educate the whole being of children so that they can build a brighter future for themselves and for the planet	

first. In this case, it is reasonable to assume few listeners need to know why creativity is as important as literacy. Sir Ken can take that as a given. The more pressing question is, "Do we actually need to teach kids the basics of how to be creative?"

In the first part of his talk (Part A in Table 2.3), Sir Ken answers this question with a definitive no. Children are born as creative beings. That is the end of the "situation" segment of his argument. However, this raises the next logical question, "Then what is the problem?" The second part of his talk lays out the complication that our current education system fosters left-brain logical development and casts aside right-brain creative expression. This raises the new question, "Well, is that necessarily a bad thing?" Still within the "complication" part of his speech, Sir Ken answers by arguing that the present system is not making us happier and more productive; quite the contrary, it is simply leading to academic inflation.

Feeling the intensity of the problem at its peak, the audience is now seeking a resolution. The third part of Sir Ken's speech reveals that our greatest hope lies in embracing the diversity of human intelligence. Though his case is complete, audiences appreciate when a speaker wraps up his conclusion in a nice little package by explicitly stating it. That is precisely what Sir Ken does with his final words:

> What TED celebrates is the gift of the human imagination. We have to be careful now that we use this gift wisely and that we avert some of the scenarios that we've talked about. And the only way we'll do it is by seeing our creative capacities for the richness they are and seeing our children for the hope that they are. And our task is to educate their whole being, so they can face this future. By the way—we may not see this future, but they will. And our job is to help them make something of it.

Many discussions of narrative structure focus less on logical argument and more on organizing patterns. Common examples include:

- *Problem-solution.* Frame the problem. Share the solution. Outline the benefits. Give the audience a call to action.

- *Alternatives.* Share the viewpoint of adherents on one side of an issue. Share the viewpoint that supports the other side. Share your more enlightened view.

- *Demonstration.* Reveal something cool. Share its features and benefits. Tell people when and how they can get one.

For persuasive talks, I prefer the "premise-proof" approach since you can still overlay any organizing pattern. For instance, Charlie Todd and Ken Robinson both used the fairly ubiquitous problem-solution pattern, but they employed different logical narrative approaches. Besides flexibility and argumentative purity, the premise-proof approach keeps your eyes focused on the big shiny object—your idea worth spreading.

Now that you have a deep understanding of the logical foundation for your speech, it is time to understand more deeply how to select and tell stories with impact.

CHAPTER 3

Telling Your Story

TIP 14: Draw stories worth telling from your personal experience.

If you would like to bore people to tears until they tear out their hair and claw their eyes out, then hammer them with facts for the entire 18 minutes of your TED Talk. Of course, the TED organizers will never let you get away with that. Every idea worth spreading must be packaged in a story worth telling. Every part of your speech— the opening, the body, and the conclusion—offers an opportunity to tell that story. You may choose to deliver a story-driven narrative by sharing a single drawn-out story. Or you may wish to tell a sequence of vignettes that serve as proof in a premise-driven narrative.

The first question that arises is which story or stories should you tell? The easy answer is that it is always best to tell stories drawn from your personal experience or observation. Imagine you chose to share the greatest lesson you ever learned. Your story becomes how and when you learned it. If you survived into adulthood, then you have countless stories of perseverance in the face of failure. You have loved and you have lost. You have harmed and you have been harmed. Ordinary lives are punctuated by extraordinary moments.

Your stories can inspire others; you just need to learn to share them with full emotional force.

At any given time, people are suffering from either story block or story overload. Those who are blocked feel that their lives are ordinary and that they have not had dramatic experiences. On deeper reflection, you will realize that is nonsense. You and I and everyone around us experience at least one epiphany per day in our amazing lives. When you tune in to your emotions moment by moment, you will see hundreds of stories dancing all around you. That degree of sensitivity leads you to story overload. You know you have contracted that condition when you try to squeeze a lifetime of insights into an 18-minute TED Talk. The panacea for both conditions is to find one story with one central theme that is deeply personal. Here are three storytelling prompts that offer an instant cure.

Prompt 1. One Lesson

If you could go back in time and give yourself one lesson, what would it be? A safe, but still impactful, approach is to give this lesson to your professional self. You probably have a bunch of lessons from which to choose, but you need to pick only one. Here is one of mine. At the beginning of my professional life I believed that the sign of true success was to be so amazing at my job that my manager would leave me alone. For an entire decade I lived in this state of ignorance until a great manager opened my eyes to the power of seeking and accepting continual feedback. Ever since then, I've wished I could have a time machine to give my younger self a swift kick in the butt.

Some people I mention this to wish they had their own time machine so that they could give their younger self a warning that would have prevented a single catastrophic event. I do not recommend that sort of lesson for a few reasons. Though you will connect with the people in your audience by showing vulnerability, you will leave them feeling bad for what happened to you. They will not be able to help you, and they will not be able to relate your warning to their own lives—which is the point of this whole thing. Instead, focus on an eternal truth. Mine is "The journey is the reward." Though that is not a novel concept, the magic is in the sharing of the story of how I felt before I embraced my truth, the experience of the exact moment I grasped its meaning, and the explanation of what my life has been like since.

Prompt 2. Defining Moment

What was *the* defining moment that most dramatically changed the course of your life? Though this could be a moment of great triumph or joy, the most powerful stories come from loss, pain, terror, or failure. Again, you can play it safe with professional stories, or you can go deep with personal ones. If you are giving a humorous speech, then choose your most embarrassing moment for your defining moment.

If you go dark and personal, remember that you need to provide relief by bringing your audience back toward light and hope. In her talk at TEDxRainier, Leslie Morgan Steiner[1] shared the idea worth spreading of helping domestic violence victims get out of their "crazy love stories" by imploring everyone to speak up about the early warning signs of abuse. Leslie alternated between horrific descriptions of being abused during her first marriage, such as having a loaded gun held to her head, and happy images of life with a loving husband in her second marriage, including mentions of her three children, a black Labrador retriever, and a Honda Odyssey minivan. Importantly, she ended her talk with an image of a world free of domestic violence where every family lives in a safe and peaceful home.

To make a good story great, frame the defining moment as a moment of choice. Choices between good and evil are too easy and too obvious. Instead, present choices between two goods, or better yet, between two evils. To add even more suspense, share how you ignored the choice for a while as your situation got even more complicated.

Prompt 3. Overcoming Weakness

What early weakness led you to find your passion? Many people develop their greatest strength fueled by the anxiety of hiding or compensating for an early perceived weakness. Most great speakers started out terrified of public speaking. Many great achievers rallied after being told by an authority figure that they would never amount to anything. I did not read my first book cover to cover until I was 15 years old, when my compassionate tenth grade English teacher, James Coats, set me on a path to becoming a voracious reader and writer. (A belated thank you to Clifton Keith Hillegass, the founder of CliffsNotes, for getting me through middle school.)

Use one of the three storytelling prompts, the one that resonates most deeply with you, to find your story worth spreading.

TIP 15: Develop your story using the hero's journey three-act structure.

If TED had been around when mythologist Joseph Campbell was alive, he would most certainly have delivered one of the most valuable talks of all time. In his groundbreaking 1949 book, *The Hero with a Thousand Faces*, Campbell formulated his idea worth spreading by combining thousands of years of important myths from around the world with the principles of modern psychology. He came up with the "monomyth," more commonly known as the hero's journey, as the fundamental storytelling pattern that transcends time, space, and culture.

Unfortunately, Mr. Campbell's book is as impenetrable as it is valuable. Luckily a number of expert screenwriters put their own interpretation on the seminal work to make its concepts accessible to mere mortals. The notable individuals who stood on the original giant's shoulders and then on each others' include Syd Field (*Screenplay*, 1979), Robert McKee (*Story*, 1997), Blake Snyder (*Save the Cat*, 2005), and Christopher Vogler (*The Writer's Journey*, 2007).

Among these, the latter two are the most readable. Read Vogler's book first to get the foundation; then read Snyder's for clever tricks and techniques that add texture.

Vogler's and Snyder's patterns are designed for creating full-length movies lasting 90 to 120 minutes or even longer. An 18-minute TED Talk simply cannot cover that much ground. However, every story must have a minimum number of elements. The "Pixar pitch" espoused by Matthew Luhn, head of story at the acclaimed animation studio, gives an excellent framework for the minimum elements required to build a compelling story. The gist of the Pixar pitch is that every one of the three acts must have a clear beginning and an end. Act I establishes the situation. Act II works through the complications. And Act III provides the resolution. Table 3.1 compares the storytelling patterns of Vogler, Snyder, and Pixar.

The best way to understand how to apply these storytelling patterns is to deconstruct a TED Talk delivered by a person well versed in the methods of weaving an inspirational hero's quest. With her generous permission, let us examine Becky Blanton's TEDGlobal 2009 talk entitled "The Year I Was Homeless"[2] through the lens of Christopher Vogler's model. Since Ms. Blanton is a journalist and an author, we are literally applying *The Writer's Journey* to the writer's journey! Let's get started.

TIP 16: Use the "Ordinary World" to introduce your protagonist and to establish your theme.

Ordinary World
I'm a writer and a journalist, and I'm also an insanely curious person, so in twenty-two years as a journalist, I've learned how to do a lot of new things.

It does not matter whether or not the people in your audience actually like your hero, but they must be able to relate to this person

TABLE 3.1

Storytelling Patterns of Christopher Vogler, Blake Snyder, and the Pixar Pitch

	VOGLER'S *THE WRITER'S JOURNEY*	SNYDER'S "BEAT SHEET"	PIXAR PITCH
Act I	Ordinary World	Opening image	Once upon a time ..., and every day ...
		Theme stated	
		Setup	
	Call to Adventure	Catalyst	... until one day ...
	Refusal of the Call	Debate	
	Meeting with the Mentor		
	Crossing the First Threshold	Break into two	
Act II	Tests, Allies, and Enemies	B story	... and because of that
		Fun and games	
	Approach to the Inmost Cave	Midpoint	... and because of that
	Ordeal	Bad guys close in	... and because of that ...
		All is lost	
		Dark night of the soul	
	Reward	Break into three	... until finally, ...
Act III	The Road Back	Finale	... and since that day ...
	Resurrection		
	Return with the Elixir	Final image	And the moral of the story is ...

in order to connect with and learn from the story. The Ordinary World offers a chance for listeners to absorb the essential details of Becky's strengths, mindset, desires, relationships, and flaws.

Since Becky had less than seven minutes to deliver her talk, she condensed her Ordinary World into a single sentence. Though she explicitly states two character strengths, curiosity and learning ability, she uses the trick of labeling herself with her profession to skip the need for additional detail. The stereotype of a modern journalist is of someone who is tough and independent but living a modest, middle-class existence. Ms. Blanton reinforced this stereotype with her simple attire consisting of a gray button-down shirt with rolled-up sleeves, a black vest, black slacks, and comfortable shoes.

So where is the tragic flaw? In many of the most textured protagonists, their primary strength is also their principal weakness. As we are about to learn, her curiosity leads her into the heart of darkness. This setup also foreshadows a core theme running through her talk—the dramatic question of whether or not it is a good idea to constantly pursue new knowledge and experiences.

TIP 17: Use the "Call to Adventure" to disrupt your hero's life and to give your hero a goal.

Call to Adventure
And three years ago, one of the things I learned how to do was to become invisible. I became one of the working homeless. I quit my job as a newspaper editor after my father died in February of that same year, and decided to travel. His death hit me pretty hard. And there were a lot of things that I wanted to feel and deal with while I was doing that.

The Call to Adventure is an internal or external catalyst that shakes your hero's world. To be realistic, the catalyst should be a direct threat to a fundamental human need and is often an outright threat to existence. External triggers threaten the bottom of Maslow's hierarchy, including physiological needs, safety needs, and relationship needs. People take extreme measures to survive and to protect the people they love. Internal disruptors that puncture self-esteem or prevent self-actualization can be equally powerful. Both internal and external calls highlight that the hero is somehow incomplete and can be motivated by overcoming loss, preventing loss, or pursuing temptations. Intense dissatisfaction with one's lot in life, for example, has cast many heroes into great adventures.

Whereas average stories have catalysts that operate on only one level, great stories have a Call to Adventure that gives the hero a strong external goal but an even stronger internal goal. Once again, Ms. Blanton does not disappoint. The loss of a family member prompts an external search for a substitute relationship. Additionally, you get a sense from "things that I wanted to feel and deal with" that there are strong internal forces at play here affecting self-esteem. Though she does not disclose it in her speech, Becky's father was an alcoholic and was physically abusive. She permitted me to share the following with you to give hope to other survivors of abuse:

> He would beat me for any reason, some reason, or no reason at all. When I was ten, he came in with a belt and I protested that I hadn't done anything. He said, "Well, you've probably done something that I didn't catch, so you're getting the belt."
>
> I don't know why I said it, but at that point I suggested, "Why don't you let me write a paper about why you shouldn't beat me." Growing up that's all he talked about was he had a paper to write; he had started college late in life. Somehow in my 10-year-old mind, I thought, "If I write a paper, then maybe I can get out of this beating." He considered it and he let me write the paper. It was the last time he ever beat me. I was writing for my life. Every time he would get drunk and pull out the belt, I'd say, "Let me write a paper about why you shouldn't do that." I learned to write persuasive papers as a child. Then that just continued.

Low-risk choices with guaranteed rewards are boring. The Call to Adventure should never be an easy choice. Instead, give your hero a tough choice between two comparable goods, or even better, between two equivalent evils. Or if the adventure offers great potential reward, it should come with low odds of success and a catastrophic cost of failure. In Ms. Blanton's case, she could stay at home with her growing depression. Or she could try to outrun it in exchange for living on the desperate edge of society.

The Call to Adventure is usually the best opportunity to introduce the villain (or to reveal that a character from the hero's Ordinary World is actually an opponent). Opponents need not be totally evil; they are the heroes of their own stories after all. Villains create conflict because they seek the same external goal and they *believe* that the death, destruction, or defeat of the hero is the only way to obtain it.

TIP 18: Raise the tension with your hero's "Refusal of the Call."

We will return to Becky's narrative in a few moments, but I need to draw your attention to a couple of story elements that she did not have time for in her short talk. This tip covers the first one, the Refusal of the Call. The next tip covers the second one, the Meeting with the Mentor. The story elements do not need to come in a precise order, nor do they all need to be present. However, if you reorder or exclude elements, you should do so with mindful awareness of the consequences.

To make a story believable, your characters must take the minimum conservative action at every point in time. Minimum does not necessarily or always mean small; individuals do take extreme measures to combat exceptional circumstances. For instance, you will jump in front of an oncoming train in order to push your child out of harm's way.

In the first episode of the 1988 PBS series *Joseph Campbell and the Power of Myth with Bill Moyers*, Campbell outlines the three types of heroes that you can create. In her story, Ms. Blanton falls into the first category—the intentional hero. This hero sets off on a quest to achieve a specific goal. In the process of attaining the goal, the hero often undergoes a psychological or spiritual transformation that is far more significant than her physical experience. Campbell's second type, the reluctant hero, is forced against her will into a journey. The example that Campbell uses is a soldier drafted into a war. A milder example, repeated frequently in modern cinema, is a child forced into a cross-country road trip with her parents. His third type, the accidental hero, is the middle ground between the intentional hero and the reluctant hero. Using her own free will, the accidental hero falls into an unexpected journey. In ancient stories, this was represented by a person following a magical animal into the forest. The movie *The Hangover* represents a more modern, comical version of this archetype with characters who start out by seeking fun but quickly find themselves in a dramatic adventure.

All three heroes, but especially the reluctant heroes, may refuse the Call to Adventure once or even multiple times. In fact, the Refusal of the Call is another powerful tension builder. The audience delights in knowing what the hero must do long before she accepts her fate. Moreover, successive refusals should make the hero's Ordinary World increasingly uninhabitable.

The hero's voice may not be the only impediment to commitment. In many stories, the hero is physically or emotionally held back by one or more threshold guardians. Though physical restraints may be fairly obvious, external emotional ones may come in many flavors. The most powerful among them are when friends, rather than enemies, cast doubt or exert social pressure to maintain the status quo.

Before they commit to their quest, even intentional heroes like Becky can refuse the Call to Adventure. However, Ms. Blanton had limited time and enough drama elsewhere in her story that she did not need to include a Refusal of the Call even though she likely had to build her resolve in real life.

TIP 19: Arrange a "Meeting with the Mentor" to keep your hero from being viewed as special.

One of the greatest mistakes that speakers can make is telling a personal story about their massive success without acknowledging the help they received along the way. By presenting themselves as so gifted, they place themselves on a pedestal relative to their audience. However, for people to be able to connect and be inspired enough to apply that wisdom to their own lives, they must feel that the process, not the speaker, is special.

One TED speaker, a writer with a runaway international bestseller, unintentionally violated this rule by mentioning her sudden success. Though she was very innocently using this as a setup for a self-deprecating joke about how she could never top this feat, the damage was done. The writer meant well; she was honestly surprised by her success, perhaps the most surprised person on the planet. The problem is that sharing her astonishment at her own success put her on a pedestal. This transgression was clearly not the end of the world, as her talk is among the most popular TED Talks; it positively affected millions of lives, including my own. However, avoid self-aggrandizement, or even the appearance of it.

The cure for this problem is to introduce one or more mentors to provide supplies, protection, and knowledge. Each of these gifts boosts a hero's ability to continue the journey into the unknown. Note that the mentor need not be a single character. It can be a temporary role that multiple characters temporarily assume. Moreover, mentors may not even be human. Other living organisms, inanimate objects, and even intangibles often serve as mentors, including animals, books, and songs, respectively.

As you will discover in Becky Blanton's story, there is no envy-evoking reward at the end of the rainbow. She positioned herself as an equal, perhaps a guide, but not as superior to her listeners. Becky shared her flaws, failures, and vulnerabilities that make her human. Consequently, her story does not include a mentor to guide her. Even if she had a mentor, every hero must ultimately face the unknown alone.

TIP 20: Make your hero commit to her journey by "Crossing the First Threshold."

Crossing the First Threshold
I've camped my whole life. And I decided that living in a van for
a year to do this would be like one long camping trip. So I packed
my cat, my Rottweiler and my camping gear into a 1975 Chevy
van, and drove off into the sunset, having fully failed to realize
three critical things. One: that society equates living in a perma-
nent structure, even a shack, with having value as a person. Two:
I failed to realize how quickly the negative perceptions of other
people can impact our reality, if we let it. Three: I failed to realize
that homelessness is an attitude, not a lifestyle.

Though the hero's journey can be purely psychological, most journeys do involve physical movement to allow the protagonist to Cross the First Threshold into an unfamiliar world. In either case, the hero must take decisive action that increases risk, involves self-sacrifice, and commits the hero to the adventure in a way that adds a noticeable increase in energy to the story.

Becky enters the special world of her story naive but not wholly unprepared. By sharing that she is an experienced camper, she gives listeners hope that she will be able to survive the coming storm.

TIP 21: Arm your hero with knowledge acquired from "Tests, Allies, and Enemies."

Tests, Allies, and Enemies
At first, living in the van was great. I showered in campgrounds. I
ate out regularly. And I had time to relax and to grieve. But then
the anger and the depression about my father's death set in. My
freelance job ended. And I had to get a full-time job to pay the bills.
What had been a really mild spring turned into a miserably hot

summer. And it became impossible to park anywhere without being very obvious that I had a cat and a dog with me, and it was really hot. The cat came and went through an open window in the van. The doggy went into doggy day care. And I sweated. Whenever I could, I used employee showers in office buildings and truck stops. Or I washed up in public restrooms.

Nighttime temperatures in the van rarely dropped below 80 degrees Fahrenheit, making it difficult or impossible to sleep. Food rotted in the heat. Ice in my ice chest melted within hours, and it was pretty miserable. I couldn't afford to find an apartment, or couldn't afford an apartment that would allow me to have the Rottweiler and the cat. And I refused to give them up, so I stayed in the van. And when the heat made me too sick to walk the 50 feet to the public restroom outside my van at night, I used a bucket and a trash bag as a toilet.

Once the hero is committed to her journey with no turning back, she learns the rules of the special world through a series of trials that are difficult but not life-threatening. The information and power she accumulates should be necessary but not sufficient to survive the ordeal ahead.

As Becky highlighted in her story, these tests create increasing emotional intensity that alternates between positive and negative. She starts out on a positive note in what amounts to a comfortable camping trip with time for emotional healing. Then her story shifts negative as she faces emotional, financial, and physical challenges. There is a small release of tension as she finds a home for her dog and discovers a way, albeit desperate, to keep clean. In her final trail, she cranks the negative intensity way up again with increasing desperation.

This phase is a time in most stories where the hero picks up friends and encounters a range of minor enemies such as the villain's henchman. In Becky's case, though she did not have time to elaborate, her friends were her pets. Becky's villains are homelessness and depression. Her bouts of depression are growing stronger, but she has not reached outright insanity.

TIP 22: Take away your hero's options in her "Approach to the Inmost Cave."

Approach to the Inmost Cave
When winter weather set in, the temperatures dropped below freezing. And they stayed there. And I faced a whole new set of challenges. I parked a different place every night so I would avoid being noticed and hassled by the police. I didn't always succeed.

But I felt out of control of my life. And I don't know when or how it happened, but the speed at which I went from being a talented writer and journalist to being a homeless woman, living in a van, took my breath away. I hadn't changed. My I.Q. hadn't dropped. My talent, my integrity, my values, everything about me remained the same. But I had changed somehow. I spiraled deeper and deeper into a depression.

In the previous phase of her story, Ms. Blanton acquired survival skills that ordinary campers never need to learn. But during the Approach to the Inmost Cave, her options become more limited both physically and emotionally. You can be miserably uncomfortable living in a van in the summer time. However, the stakes are much higher with freezing winter temperatures. With the added adversary of the police, Ms. Blanton fell deeper into the depths of depression. She was trapped and facing the only possible exit, the mouth of the cave, the great unknown.

TIP 23: Subject your hero to a life-or-death "Ordeal."

Ordeal
And eventually someone referred me to a homeless health clinic. And I went. I hadn't bathed in three days. I was as smelly and as depressed as anyone in line. I just wasn't drunk or high. And when several of the homeless men realized that, including a former

university professor, they said, "You aren't homeless. Why are you really here?" Other homeless people didn't see me as homeless, but I did. Then the professor listened to my story and he said, "You have a job. You have hope. The real homeless don't have hope." A reaction to the medication the clinic gave me for my depression left me suicidal. And I remember thinking, "If I killed myself, no one would notice."

In Christopher Vogler's writer's journey model, heroes must face two brushes with their greatest fear. The Ordeal is the first brush, which he refers to as a crisis but not a climax. Common crises might be a near-death experience for the hero, the death of a mentor, the tragic end of a life-giving relationship, or utter financial ruin. Becky's situation, contemplating suicide, fits the first and most dramatic type of crisis.

Physical and emotional Ordeals challenge the hero. An environment that Becky thought would be her greatest hope—a homeless health clinic—actually turned out to be her greatest nightmare. Her supposed allies, healthcare workers and other homeless people, did not accept her as one of their own. This unexpected twist, or misdirection of the listener's expectations, fuels the intensity of this crisis and further transforms her views of homelessness and society.

TIP 24: "Reward" your hero for surviving her first major crisis.

Reward
A friend told me, shortly after that, that she had heard that Tim Russert, a nationally renowned journalist, had been talking about me on national T.V. An essay I'd written about my father, the year before he died, was in Tim's new book. And he was doing the talk show circuit. And he was talking about my writing. And when I

realized that Tim Russert, former moderator of Meet the Press, *was talking about my writing, while I was living in a van in a Wal-Mart parking lot, I started laughing. You should too.*

I started laughing because it got to the point where, was I a writer, or was I a homeless woman? So I went in the bookstore. And I found Tim's book. And I stood there. And I reread my essay. And I cried. Because I was a writer. I was a writer.

Exhausted after their Ordeal, heroes take at least temporary possession of one of the rewards they were seeking, often their external goal. This allows them to recuperate and to experience a catharsis, or emotional release, frequently accompanied by crying or laughter. Becky experiences a dramatic and complete catharsis. Russert's book containing her essay, the reward, helps her laugh and cry.

TIP 25: Start your hero on "the Road Back" to a normal life.

The Road Back
Shortly after that I moved back to Tennessee. I alternated between living in a van and couch surfing with friends. And I started writing again.

With their energy replenished, heroes make the active choice to leave the depths of the special world and make their way either back to their original home or onward to a new home. In longer stories, especially those with human opponents, the road back involves a flight from the villain's lair or the pursuit of an escaped villain. Since that road is paved with danger, the path leads to a catastrophic reversal of the hero's recent good fortune. Becky traveled a literal road—one that led her back to Tennessee. And though lacking dramatic detail, you get the sense that she was not yet completely out of danger; she was still technically homeless.

TIP 26: Follow the climax of your story with the hero's "Resurrection."

Resurrection
By the summer of the following year I was a working journalist.
I was winning awards. I was living in my own apartment. I was
no longer homeless. And I was no longer invisible.

The Resurrection is Vogler's label for the hero's ultimate brush with death and her immediate victory. It is the climax of the story. Ms. Blanton opted for what Mr. Vogler refers to as a "quiet climax." It is so quiet, in fact, that the listener needs to infer Becky's slow road to recovery. If she had more time, she could have filled in the details. Instead, she used her words to describe the aftermath.

One of Christopher Vogler's principles is that the reward should be proportionate to the sacrifice. She ended her journey with a normal life, a job with a healthy degree of recognition, and a place to live. If she had ended up a millionaire and winner of the Nobel Prize for Literature, her climax would have needed to be far more dramatic.

TIP 27: Embed your idea worth spreading in the hero's ultimate "Return with the Elixir."

Return with the Elixir
Thousands of people work full- and part-time jobs, and live in
their cars. But society continues to stigmatize and criminalize liv-
ing in your vehicle or on the streets. So the homeless, the working
homeless, primarily remain invisible. But if you ever meet one,
engage them, encourage them, and offer them hope. The human
spirit can overcome anything if it has hope.
*   And I'm not here to be the poster girl for the homeless. I'm*
not here to encourage you to give money to the next panhandler

you meet. But I am here to tell you that, based on my experience, people are not where they live, where they sleep, or what their life situation is at any given time.

Three years ago I was living in a van in a Wal-Mart parking lot, and today I'm speaking at TED. Hope always, always, finds a way. Thank you.

In the final stage, the hero returns with treasures such as love, freedom, knowledge, or wealth. These gifts can be shared with others to improve their lives. In a TED Talk, the elixir is quite naturally an idea worth spreading. By listening to her story, the people in her audience met a homeless person—something that most people of even modest privilege never do. In the process, they learned not to judge a book by its cover.

Every story should have a complete positive or negative ending. (Yes, a cliff-hanger is the third option, but that is best saved for movies with planned sequels.) Stories with positive endings are highly effective for inspiration. They make people believe, "I can do that." In contrast, cautionary tales are more effective for teaching. Since pleasure is a more powerful long-term motivation than pain, I recommend telling stories with positive endings the vast majority of the time. Your story's conclusion is your opportunity to transfer wisdom. Ending with your own emotional disclosure adds additional depth to your story.

The time to pull out the calamity tale is when you are trying to instill the virtues of safety in audiences who work in dangerous professions like construction or law enforcement. Nothing says "Pay attention" more than "Listen up, or you might be the next one to die in a careless, preventable accident." If you do relate a story that ends in disaster, spend time at the end exploring ways that the characters could have avoided their fate.

Above all, you will be far more successful with upbeat stories than with negative ones, even in an environment of disillusionment; if applicable, first acknowledge what is wrong, and then move toward positive outcomes. People crave speakers and stories that are authentic, yes, but also passionate and fun.

The mark of a great story is that it allows the listener to discover layer upon layer of wisdom through interpretation. This subtlety lies in not being overtly outcome focused. To enable the listener to peel the onion, you must make your stories rich in personal, emotional content as well as vivid sensory detail. Stories need not be objective or balanced. In fact, the most compelling stories are told from a subjective point of view. You need your emotions to shine through, and that can only be achieved if you express your most strongly held beliefs.

TIP 28: Bring your characters to life on stage with physical appearance and dialogue.

The golden rule of storytelling is "Show, don't tell." Another way to say this is that you need to relive, not retell, your story by re-creating your experiences on the stage. The image this conveys should include authentic characters revealed through dialogue and physical appearance.

Authentic characters, with all their warts and complexity, are the basis for any riveting story. By identifying with specific character traits, listeners imagine themselves and people they care about as the protagonists. Invite the audience into your story to relive it with you by reenacting characters and their reactions. This encompasses what is seen, including posture and gestures; what is heard, the tone of voice; and what is implied, character traits and desires.

Unless you have theatrical experience, doing this will be unfamiliar at first and uncomfortable on stage. The key is not to overthink but simply to channel the distinct personality of the individual characters as you shine a virtual spotlight on them in your story. You can also take solace in the fact that there is no "right" or "perfect" amount of dramatic performance. By cranking up the volume to the level that you are comfortable with but not beyond, you will remain authentic.

Instead of merely narrating what the characters do, give them dynamic, conversational dialogue. When dialogue explicitly tells what a character is thinking, doing, or feeling, then it is not realistic. Think about how people converse. Real dialogue gets right to the point. It achieves verisimilitude with contractions, partial sentences, and even the occasional "um," "like," or "you know." It conveys emotion. Though dialogue can be used (very sparingly) to share information, its primary purpose is either to move the story forward or to contribute to revealing a character's strengths, flaws, and desires.

Real dialogue is more powerful when it conveys the subtext, or deeper meaning, of a character's true emotions and desires. In an effort to protect their egos from humiliation, characters are at the very least vague and often make statements that are contradictory to what they actually want. In addition to beating around the bush and lying, the other common form of subtext-laden dialogue involves characters discussing a topic that serves as a symbolic or metaphorical representation of a looming, unspoken issue.

Within reason, each character should have a distinct speech pattern or voice. Drawing on stereotypes, less-educated characters might speak more slowly and with less-than-crisp enunciation. If the speaker is a woman, she might adopt a lower pitch when delivering male dialogue. If a character is older, then the voice may be slightly gruffer. Sometimes a regional accent is appropriate. This paragraph was intentionally started with the phrase *within reason*. In most dialogue, each character's voice needs only to be tailored enough to be distinct. The exception, of course, is for over-the-top characters who are used for comic relief.

Your characters should also have fixed stage locations. When you embody a particular character, go stand in his or her assigned spot on the stage. When you need to narrate, an effective technique is to step forward toward the audience and then step back when you resume character.

TIP 29: Bring your audience into your setting.

Perhaps the biggest mistake speakers make when recounting stories is being too vague about the setting. To be realistic and allow the audience to relive the story, the setting must be specific in time, location, and atmosphere.

Either by nature or by the conditioning of having grown up with fairy tales that begin "Once upon a time . . . ," listeners need to be able to place your story in historical context. This should be done very early on, usually with your very first words. Ms. Blanton got there in her second sentence, "And three years ago . . ." Well-told stories also need to clearly signal the passage of time. In addition to references to the passing of seasons, Becky employed other cues, including "Eventually . . ." and "Shortly after that . . ." Though these latter references were vague, the audience never felt lost in time.

Ms. Blanton also provided strong sensory descriptions of her settings, including the inside of her 1975 Chevy van, a homeless health clinic, and a bookstore. Settings can engage every sense: sight, sound, smell, touch, and even taste. However, it is important to be subtle about this. Avoid engaging every sense all at once since that will take your prose from being sophisticated to being flowery. Though knowing the color of the van might have helped (it was green by the way), it is enough for the audience to know that Ms. Blanton was trapped in a vehicle more than 30 years old. Listeners can visualize its boxy, rusted, and dented exterior. Similarly, she does not need to describe the smells or the sounds of living with a cat and a large dog in a confined space—that is best left to the imagination.

Atmosphere, the final element of setting, is the key to establishing the mood. Seasons, weather, lighting, and even physical objects carry built-in moods that help the speaker establish setting with fewer words.

TIP 30: Apply the hero's journey framework to stories about others.

I may have given you the impression that you have to tell a gripping, life-or-death personal story. However, there are plenty of great TED Talks in which the speaker tells someone else's story. A good example is when speakers bring stories of esoteric academic or industrial research to life.

Malcolm Gladwell, author of *Blink* and *Tipping Point* and all-around chronicler of pop psychology, did this in his famous "Choice, Happiness and Spaghetti Sauce"[3] speech. His idea worth spreading is "to embrace the diversity of human beings so that human beings can be happier." Stated another way, people do not want spaghetti sauce; they want spaghetti sauces. To prove the point, Mr. Gladwell shared a story about revolutionary food scientist Howard Moscowitz. The premise-proof outline for Mr. Gladwell's talk is shown in Table 3.2.

Malcolm Gladwell's speech is highly complex in its construction for a couple of reasons. First, he tells complete substories within his primary story. Second, he does not consistently provide a concrete statement of the premises that listeners should draw from his deductive premise chain. To see this, we will deconstruct his talk using the Pixar pitch framework originally shown in Table 3.1 and the premise chain analysis technique. In the process, you will find that most of the classic elements of the hero's journey are present in Mr. Gladwell's talk.

> Act I. *Once upon a time*, there was a Harvard-educated food scientist named Howard Moscowitz. *And every day*, Howard liked to measure things in his little consulting shop in White Plains, New York. *Until one day* PepsiCo hired him to determine how much artificial sweetener to add to Diet Pepsi. While struggling to make sense of the data he had captured, he had an epiphany—"They were asking the wrong question. They were looking

TABLE 3.2

Outline of Malcolm Gladwell's "Choice, Happiness and Spaghetti Sauce" TED Talk

ELEMENT	PREMISE	PROOF
Introduction	(1) Introduce Howard Moscowitz, including his personality, appearance, and profession	
Part A	(3) There is no single, "perfect" level of sweetness in a soft drink or flavor of a pickle	(2a) Aspartame in Diet Pepsi story (2b) Perfect Vlasic pickle story
Part B	(5) In fact, there is no single, "perfect" food formulation of almost any kind	(4a) Prego versus Ragú spaghetti sauce story (4b) References to vinegar, mustard, and olive oil
Part C	(7) People cannot express what they want. However, if you observe them, you find that different people have different tastes. Hence, there is no single food that achieves Platonic perfection	(6a) Spaghetti sauce focus groups (6b) Rich versus weak coffee example (6c) Grey Poupon mustard story (6d) Shift from scientific quest for universals to study of variability
Conclusion	(9) We find a surer way to true happiness by embracing the diversity of human beings	(8) Nescafé coffee story

for the perfect Pepsi, and they should have been looking for the perfect Pepsis." But PepsiCo and everyone else thought he was crazy.

Act II. *And because of that*, he tried to prove he was not crazy by revealing the same insight about pickles, but the food industry still would not listen. *And because of that*, he applied his theory of taste diversity to spaghetti sauce. *Until finally* Campbell's, the maker of Prego spaghetti sauce, made hundreds of millions of dollars from his idea.

Act III. *And since that day*, Dr. Moscowitz's finding has been applied in scores of industries, including mustards, vinegars, olive oils, and coffees, with similar benefits to companies and consumers. *And the moral of the story is* "that in embracing the diversity of human beings, we will find a surer way to true happiness."

Mr. Gladwell embedded complete substories within his overall story, a sophisticated technique borrowed from fiction and film. Though often executed in the form of a flashback, this technique can also be used as Malcolm did in the ordinary chronological flow of story. You can see it in the following example, where the spaghetti sauce substory is broken down using the Pixar pitch framework. Notice that Mr. Gladwell shifts the point of view from Howard Moscowitz as the protagonist to Campbell's Soup as the hero.

Act I. *Once upon a time*, in the early 1980s, Campbell's Soup was losing the battle of its technically superior (according to Mr. Gladwell, who referenced the famous bowl test back in the 1970s) Prego spaghetti sauce against its rival Ragú. *Until one day*, the company hired Howard Moscowitz to fix its product line.

Act II. *And because of that*, Howard formulated 45 varieties of spaghetti sauce. *And because of that*, he collected data on taste preferences of "people by the truckload." *Until finally*, he discovered that Americans fall into three clusters: "There are people who like their spaghetti sauce plain; there are people who like their spaghetti sauce spicy; and there are people who like it extra chunky."

Act III. *And since that day*, Campbell's "completely took over the spaghetti sauce business in this country. And over the next 10 years, they made 600 million dollars off their line of extra-chunky sauces." *And the moral of the story is* that variety is both profitable and delightful.

As a side note, Mr. Gladwell's story-within-a-story construction is further complicated or enhanced, depending on your perspective, by his frequent use of foreshadowing. For example, he makes a brief foreshadowing reference to Nescafé during his early Diet Pepsi story before returning in depth to coffee variety two more times. He does this again when mentioning mustard during his spaghetti sauce story only to return to it in full detail later in his Grey Poupon story.

Mr. Gladwell artfully weaves his deductive premise chain into the fabric of his story. His chain begins with the factually proven statement that there is no perfect Pepsi or perfect pickle. This prompts the question, "Is there any perfect food?" to which Mr. Gladwell responds with a definitive no because you observe the same phenomenon for a variety of other foods. Since this does not answer the last question beyond a shadow of a doubt, listeners ask, "But why do you know this applies to all foods?" The logic continues, because people cannot express what they want. However, if you observe them, you find that different people have different tastes. Hence, there is no single food that achieves Platonic perfection. The audience's final question is, "Hmmm, does this variety theory have implications beyond food science?" Again, Malcolm Gladwell responds with his ultimate message "that in embracing the diversity of human beings, we will find a surer way to true happiness."

TIP 31: Combine related observations from your personal experiences into an idea worth spreading.

Becky Blanton and Jill Bolte Taylor[4] each shared TED Talks that comprised a single personal story. There is no weave of premise and proof; instead, each speaker ended with a strong, audience-directed moral. However, many speakers mix independent personal vignettes with logical reasoning. Fashion model Cameron Russell's[5] talk illustrates this approach, as shown in Table 3.3.

In her introduction, Ms. Russell cuts right to the chase with her core message that image, though superficial, has a powerful impact on our lives. Her message is accompanied by a demonstration in which she trades high heels for flats and covers her skin-tight black minidress with an ankle-length skirt and comfortable sweater. Cameron's outfit change is meant to illustrate how looks, as well as people's perceptions, can be transformed in the blink of an eye.

The body of her speech uses the clever approach of raising the five most common questions she gets about her uncommon career choice. This is an inductive premise group consisting of five "reasons" why image is superficial yet powerful. Each of her answers is humble and counterintuitive. She enhances her answers with personal vignettes supported by photographic proof. Additionally, she bolsters two parts of her case with academic research on model ethnicity and police statistics on the impact of the "stop-and-frisk" policy on young black and Latino men in New York City.

Since Ms. Russell began her talk with her idea worth spreading, she repeats and relates it to every listener at the end. Having proved that image is powerful and superficial, she gives her audience a booster shot of self-compassion:

If there's a takeaway to this talk, I hope it's that we all feel more comfortable acknowledging the power of image in our perceived successes and our perceived failures.

TABLE 3.3

Outline of Cameron Russell's "Looks Aren't Everything. Believe Me, I'm a Model" TED Talk

ELEMENT	PREMISE	PROOF
Introduction	(2) Image, though superficial, has a powerful impact on our lives	(1) Outfit change
Part A	(3) How do you become a model? By winning the genetic lottery	(4) NYU study showing less than 4% of runway models are nonwhite
Part B	(5) Can I be a model when I grow up? Don't bother	(6) Even the fashion photographer is more "in charge" of her career than the model
Part C	(7) "Do they retouch all the photos?" Yes, and that is only the beginning of the fiction	(8) Before and after examples of fashion photography
Part D	(9) "Do you get free stuff?" Yes, and the inequality is widened by intangible benefits	(10) Stop-and-frisk practice of the New York City police
Part E	(11) "What is it like to be a model?" Not a blissful life	(12) The most beautiful models are the most physically insecure women on the planet
Conclusion	(13) To acknowledge the power of image in our perceived successes and our perceived failures so that we are more secure in our own skin	

The last two chapters explored premise-dominated and story-dominated TED Talk narratives. In between these two extremes lie the balanced narratives that are most commonly found when a speaker tells a story about someone else.

Combinations of logical argument and story are the key ingredients in crafting an effective speech. Moreover, the "To (action) so that (outcome)" phrasing is a great way to encapsulate your central message as you construct your talk. However, it is not the most elegant way of putting words together. The next chapter focuses on how to make your worthy idea more spreadable.

CHAPTER 4

Crafting Your Catchphrase

TIP 32: **Encapsulate your idea worth spreading in a viral catchphrase.**

In his TEDxPugetSound talk, Simon Sinek[1] shared a revelation that he had a few years before. He figured out the common thread that explains why some leaders and some companies succeed while others fail. Fortunately, he did not keep this to himself; after all, his life's purpose is to "inspire others so that they can do the things that inspire them."

Simon's secret, which he shares freely with the world, is expressed in his Golden Circle concept. Simon builds a compelling case that average people and average companies start with what they do, and if we are lucky, they share a little bit of how they do it. In contrast, inspiring leaders and remarkable companies first share why they do what they do; then they share how they do what they do. They save what they do for last. One of Sinek's favorite examples is Apple Computer, Inc. Apple's why is to empower individuals to challenge the status quo. Its how is by designing great physical and digital experiences at a cost affordable to the mainstream consumer. What Apple does is make computers and smartphones in various sizes, shapes, and colors.

Simon's concept is not new; it was the foundation of the mission statement fad that was all the rage decades ago. He breathed new life into an old concept and inspired millions by communicating his message in a new way with fresh stories. Simon's first masterstroke was to encapsulate this concept in the elegant Golden Circle. Think of an archery target with the "what" in the outer ring, "how" in the middle ring, and "why" in the center ring. Great communicators work from the inside ring out.

Though the phrase *the Golden Circle* is clever, it is not viral. Imagine that someone walks up to you and says, "Hey, do you want the secret to success in business and life?" As you stand ready to absorb the wisdom of the ages, he adds, "It's simple. It's the Golden Circle!" You are going to be pretty disappointed. Without further explanation, a Golden Circle has little meaning. It is not going to call you to action or change your perspective.

But Mr. Sinek pulled out a new trick in his TED Talk, the full outline of which is shown in Table 4.1. He encapsulated his concept in an unforgettable catchphrase, "Start with why." This, by the way, is also the title of his *New York Times* bestselling book, which expands on the theme of his TED Talk. Those three words tell you unambiguously what you need to do right now to become a more inspiring leader.

TIP 33: Keep your catchphrase between 3 and 12 words.

What makes a great catchphrase? For one thing, it should be short. It's best to keep it at 3 words, but you can get away with up to 12.

TABLE 4.1

Outline of Simon Sinek's "Start with Why" TED Talk

ELEMENT	PREMISE	PROOF
Introduction	(2) All great leaders and great organizations communicate from the inside out; they start with why, then share how, and finally reveal what	(1) Series of questions introducing Apple Computer, the Wright brothers, and Martin Luther King, Jr.
Part A	(4) People don't buy what you do; they buy why you do it. Therefore, you should strive to do business with people who believe what you believe	(3a) "Anti-Apple" versus Apple (3b) Golden Circle is supported by brain biology and function
Part B	(6) Some of the people who believe what you believe will work for you with their blood, sweat, and tears	(5) Samuel Pierpont Langley versus the Wright brothers
Part C	(8) People who believe what you believe will attract enough like-minded people to get you to the tipping point of the diffusion of innovation that leads to mass market acceptance	(7) TiVo versus Martin Luther King, Jr.
Conclusion	(10) It is not about the leader; it is about the people. Leaders who start with why have the ability to inspire because the people who follow do so on their own behalf	(9) Today's politicians versus leaders who start with why

In his talk, Simon actually used three catchphrases. The first one was 12 words: "People don't buy what you do; they buy why you do it." His second was 6 words: "[Sell to, hire, and attract] people who believe what you believe." And of course his stickiest one of all, "Start with why," was only three words and is a succinct reduction of "to encourage leaders to start with why [then share how and finally reveal what], so that they can inspire others."

This approach works in every realm of public speaking, including politics. Conjure up President Obama because this is his go-to recipe for sticky catchphrase pudding: "Hope and change," "Pass this bill," "We can't wait," "Yes we can."

TIP 34: Make your catchphrase action centric so that your listeners know what to do.

The second defining characteristic of sticky catchphrases is that they issue a clear call to action. Many, including "Start with why," begin with a verb. Though clichéd in certain contexts, the following mantras have the same construction: "Follow your bliss," "Seize the day," and "Speak the truth."

Catchphrases of any length can be action centric. Consider Simon's longest catchphrase, "People don't buy what you do; they buy why you do it." Though not action centric on the part of the audience (which would be better), this expression does create an image of people in action.

When you construct a two-part catchphrase, always make the second part a positive contrast to the first part. Just like in humor, put the punch word or punch phrase at the end. "People don't buy what you do" is a negative statement that triggers one's brain to ask, "Well then, what do they buy?" "They buy why you do it" satisfies the listener's immediate need to know. If Simon had said, "People buy why you do it; they don't buy what you do," it would not have had the same oomph.

TIP 35: Make your catchphrase rhythmic.

Mr. Sinek's observation "People don't buy what you do" shares the third key characteristic of power bites. They have a melodic, often rhyming, quality that makes them catchy. To truly understand that particular nearly rhyming "quality" requires a brief grammar lesson (I promise to make it as painless as possible). To make a phrase musical, you can repeat a word or phrase at the beginning (*anaphora*) or the end (*epistrophe*) of successive clauses. Dickens hammered his readers with anaphora at the beginning of the *Tale of Two Cities*:

> *It was the best of times, it was the worst of times, it was the age of wisdom, it was the age of foolishness, it was the epoch of belief, it was the epoch of incredulity, it was the season of Light, it was the season of Darkness, it was the spring of hope, it was the winter of despair, we had everything before us, we had nothing before us, we were all going direct to Heaven, we were all going direct the other way—in short, the period was so far like the present period, that some of its noisiest authorities insisted on its being received, for good or for evil, in the superlative degree of comparison only.*

So that you do not get too carried away, take note of the fact that most people can really only remember the first bit: "It was the best of times, it was the worst of times." That is the upper bound of the 3- to 12-words rule of thumb you encountered earlier. If you want to get fancy, try *symploce*, which is the combination of anaphora and epistrophe. In plain language, symploce is repeating words or phrases at the beginning as well as repeating (generally different) words or phrases at the end of successive clauses. Simon Sinek's "People don't buy what you do; they buy why you do it" uses yet another rhetorical weapon, *traductio*. This is simply repetition of the same word in different parts of the sentence.

If all that was too much, then just resort to the old standby and rhyme your catchphrase.

TIP 36: Repeat your catchphrase at least three times.

A well-built catchphrase is a short, action-centric, and rhythmic distillation of your idea worth spreading. As such, it is something that you want to implant in the minds of your listeners by repeating it at least three times. Most speakers state their catchphrase at the beginning, middle, and end of their talk.

Simon Sinek repeated his two longer catchphrases more than six times each. It is noteworthy that Simon shares his most powerful catchphrase, the one that has come to define him, "Start with why," only once and in his very last sentence:

> And it is those who start with why that have the ability to inspire those around them or find others who inspire them.

I have to imagine that if Simon had realized the phrase would become so viral, he would have repeated his other phrases less if at all, and he would have used "Start with why" six or seven times instead.

With a compelling, laser-focused single unifying message packaged into a catchphrase that makes it viral, you will have entered the upper echelon of speakers. Next, we turn to building out your speech.

CHAPTER 5

Opening Your Talk

TIP 37: Hook and guide your audience in your opening.

In literature, structure is a liberating force for creativity, rather than a limiting constraint. This is evident in the five-seven-five rhythm of the haiku and in the sonnet form, which both give rise to infinite beauty and variation. I feel that the same phenomenon holds true in the world of speechcraft. There should always be a clear opening, body, and conclusion. The art is in how the speaker fills the canvas.

Remember that the first minute or two, perhaps even the first 10 or 20 seconds of your speech, is the peak of your audience's engagement level. It is not going to get any better as one by one your listeners become distracted by their mental grocery lists. The techniques outlined below satisfy a checklist of goals you need to accomplish in your introduction:

- Hook your audience fast by stating or implying the benefits that listeners will get by paying attention to what you have to say. The most compelling benefits inform people about issues that matter to them and make them healthier, happier, or more successful.

- Develop an emotional bond with your audience. Such bonds can be formed in many ways, but opening with authenticity and showing vulnerability are the most effective.

- Get a laugh.

- Make your theme clear and either set up or reveal your idea worth spreading.

- Give your audience a sense of how your talk is structured. Rather than providing a complete overview, let the members of your audience know what signposts will signal transitions and how many they should expect to create a sense of progress. For example, you might say, "I'm going to answer the three questions that I am asked most often about what it is like being a paleontologist."

TIP 38: Begin with a prologue when the energy in your speech does not match the energy in the room.

In 9 out of 10 times, you will want to go right into your speech. Other times you need to do something different, and whichever starting point you choose has everything to do with the level of energy you sense in the room. World-class speakers strive to mirror this energy at the opening of their talk and then lead their audience on an emotional journey for the remainder. However, sometimes when there is too much or too little tension, the speaker needs to pull out a prologue. In literature and theater, a prologue gives critical details—a back story—concerning the characters and the setting that are necessary for the audience to pick up the plot at full speed.

I presume that when Sir Ken Robinson[1] delivered his TED Talk on education reform, the audience was restless after hours or days of sitting and listening to a number of presenters at the TED2006 Conference. Even being relentlessly inspired can be pretty taxing.

Consequently, he was facing a tense audience. He used the following humorous prologue as a release valve. If you are delivering a funny speech, it is critically important to get a contextually relevant laugh in the first 30 seconds to prime the audience. It took Ken Robinson less than 10:

> *Good morning. How are you? It's been great, hasn't it? I've been blown away by the whole thing. In fact, I'm leaving. [Laughter] There have been three themes, haven't there, running through the conference, which are relevant to what I want to talk about. One is the extraordinary evidence of human creativity in all of the presentations that we've had and in all of the people here. Just the variety of it and the range of it. The second is that it's put us in a place where we have no idea what's going to happen, in terms of the future. No idea how this may play out . . .*

Mr. Robinson not only used humor, but also employed another technique to connect with his audience—a technique called an opening callback. Typically, you encounter a callback when stand-up comics close their set by referring to an earlier joke or theme that had the audience in stitches. The opening callback in a keynote speech provides connective tissue between your material and the material of previous speakers. If there were no prior speakers, your opening callback could reference current events, audience members you met just before taking the stage, or conditions in the room. The opening callback should have an impromptu feel to it. Like Sir Ken Robinson's, it should be personalized for the listeners, thus making them feel that they are special and that the talk you are about to give was custom-crafted just for them.

Sir Ken Robinson uses prologues when he speaks in order to fall into rhythm with his audience. During his TED Talk, he mentioned a forthcoming book, tentatively titled *Epiphany*, based on interviews with successful people who found their talent. Released three years later, the book was ultimately titled *The Element: How*

Finding Your Passion Changes Everything. The book provides the following glimpse into why Mr. Robinson values the prologue:

> *When I am deep in the throes of exploring and presenting ideas with groups, time tends to move more quickly, more fluidly. I can be in a room with ten or twenty people or several thousand, and it's always the same. For the first five or ten minutes, I'm feeling for the energy of the room and trying things out to catch the right wavelength there. Those first minutes can feel slow. But then, when I do make the connection, I slip into a different gear.*

A prologue of extended silence can be used when there is too little tension. That can happen if you are going to give a very serious talk and the audience does not know what is coming. But this is so rare that I have never seen it used in a TED Talk—most speeches have a good title and description of which the audience is aware. However, I have seen this technique used in other forums. Ed Tate, Toastmasters World Champion of Public Speaking in 2000, is a master of this technique. An African American, Ed precedes a powerful personal story of his experiences as the target of racial hatred with a very long silence. In fact, he stands quiet and motionless for 10 full seconds before screaming a racial expletive. If 10 seconds does not sound like a long time, try it out in front of an audience; it is an eternity of silence and discomfort for you and for the audience. It is also the most amazing tension builder in a speaker's toolbox. Use it sparingly.

Another interesting prologue technique is to ask the people in your audience to imagine themselves in a particular situation or environment. This makes your talk immediately, personally, and emotionally relevant to each listener. Before sharing the story about how he studied the way his newborn son acquired language, MIT researcher Deb Roy[2] invited his TED2011 audience to imagine life inside a novel social experiment (the talk is outlined in Table 5.1):

TABLE 5.1

Outline of Deb Roy's "The Birth of a Word" TED Talk

ELEMENT	PREMISE	PROOF
Introduction	(1a) Prologue: Imagine if you could record your life … (1b) I put cameras in every room of my house and filmed for 8 to 10 hours a day, every day, for 3 years to learn the process of how children learn language	
Part A	(3) Caregiver speech complexity must drop to a minimum and then ascend with the child's ability	(2) My son learned to say *water* over the course of 18 months starting with *gagagagagaga*
Part B	(5) Sensory context is critical for language development	(4) Use of the word *water* correlates with high activity in the kitchen
Part C	(7) Growing digital tracking opens new possibilities for understanding and applying the connection between content and context	(6) Content consumption, such as television, drives social media conversations, which drives more consumption
Conclusion	(8) Video of his son's first steps	

Imagine if you could record your life—everything you said, everything you did, available in a perfect memory store at your fingertips, so you could go back and find memorable moments and relive them, or sift through traces of time and discover patterns in your own life that previously had gone undiscovered. Well that's exactly the journey that my family began five and a half years ago.

TIP 39: Start with a story when your speech is emotional and entertaining.

There are countless ways to begin your speech, and I am going to detail the three most compelling types of openings that TED speakers use to engage their audiences. Of the three, the most consistently successful opening is the story.

Here is a distilled version of what you need to know about story-based openings. First, your story should be personal. Tell your own story and share your observations. It is a good idea to make others the heroes in your stories. Second, make sure your story is directly relevant to your core message. Third, fourth, and fifth, make your story highly emotional, highly sensory, and rich in dialogue. The story should be so specific that your audience is able to relive it with you.

In his TED Talk, author and success expert Richard St. John[3] demonstrated the power of using a personal story for his opening:

> *This is really a two-hour presentation I give to high school students, cut down to three minutes. And it all started one day on a plane, on my way to TED, seven years ago. And in the seat next to me was a high school student, a teenager, and she came from a really poor family. And she wanted to make something of her life, and she asked me a simple little question. She said, "What leads to success?" And I felt really badly, because I couldn't give her a good answer. So I get off the plane, and I come to TED. And I think, jeez, I'm in the middle of a room of successful people! So why don't I ask them what helped them succeed, and pass it on to kids?*

Did you visualize yourself on that plane? Did you turn your head and eavesdrop when the teenage girl from a poor family asked Richard for the secret of success? Could you feel Richard's disappointment about not having a good answer and his zeal to be ready to help kids in the future? Moreover, and more selfishly, are you now intensely curious about what Richard St. John found to be the key to success?

Note that Richard St. John was giving a super-short TED Talk, just 3 minutes compared with the TED maximum of 18 minutes. If he had more time, then he could have added much more detail and

TABLE 5.2

Outline of Richard St. John's "8 Secrets of Success" TED Talk

ELEMENT	PREMISE	PROOF
Introduction	(1) I was sitting on a plane on my way to TED when a high school student asked, "What leads to success?" and I could not answer. So I spent seven years doing 500 interviews to answer her.	
Part A	(2) Passion	(3) Quotes by Freeman Thomas and Carol Coletta
Part B	(4) Hard work	(5) Quote by Rupert Murdoch
Part C	(6) Improve through practice	(7) Quote by Alex Garden
Part D	(9) Focus	(8) Quote by Norman Jewison
Part E	(11) "Push" through self-doubt and fatigue	(10) Quotes by David Gallo, Goldie Hawn, and Frank Gehry
Part F	(13) Service to others	(12) Quote by Sherwin Nuland
Part G	(15) Ideas	(14) Quote by Bill Gates
Part H	(17) Persistence	(16) Quote by Joe Kraus
Conclusion	(18) Do those eight things and you will succeed	

dialogue. What was the girl's name? What did she look like? How did this seemingly awkward conversation between an unaccompanied minor and businessman in his forties get started? Choose the right amount of detail for the time allotted, just as Richard did.

The outline of Richard St. John's talk is provided in Table 5.2. His TED Talk gives a taste of his extensive research on personal and professional achievement. I recommend that you read his book *8 to Be Great: The Eight Traits Successful People Have in Common* to get the full flavor of his research-based insight.

TIP 40: Start with a shocking statement to catalyze your audience.

In terms of effectiveness, there are two other types of powerful openings besides starting with a story, and they each pack an equally strong punch. Let me address the shocking statement first. Though shocking statements most frequently rely on statistics, they can also express strong opinions that challenge conventional wisdom. The important thing is that your point must trigger a range of audience emotions. If you share a what, then people will have a burning need to fill in the gaps on why, how, when, and where. In his TED2010 talk, celebrity chef and child nutrition advocate Jamie Oliver[4] used exactly this recipe in his opening. The outline for his talk is shown in Table 5.3. He started by saying:

> *Sadly, in the next eighteen minutes when I do our chat, four Americans that are alive will be dead from the food that they eat. My name is Jamie Oliver. I am thirty-four years old. I am from Essex in England and for the last seven years I have worked fairly tirelessly to save lives in my own way. I am not a doctor; I'm a chef. I don't have expensive equipment, or medicine. I use information and education. I profoundly believe that the power of food has a primal place in our homes that binds us to the best bits of life.*

Chef Oliver captured his audience by revealing a shocking truth: people are dropping like flies from the food they eat. And not half-way around the world in developing countries but in the United States. Most of the people in the audience probably wondered if they would survive lunch! Such is the power of a shocking statistic that is deeply and personally relevant to an audience. Survival is the most basic human need. Jamie went primal, life and death, and had his audience waiting with bated breath to find out why this was happening and how to stay alive.

TABLE 5.3

Outline of Jamie Oliver's "Teach Every Child About Food" TED Talk

ELEMENT	PREMISE	PROOF
Introduction	(2) Let's start a "food revolution" in America to reverse the global obesity epidemic	(1a) Diet-related disease is the biggest killer in the United States (1b) The obesity epidemic has spread to many other countries
Part A	(4) Obesity is a preventable disease	(3) Stories of suffering in Huntington, West Virginia
Part B	(6) The root of the obesity problem is: (a) Processed foods (b) Lack of cooking knowledge	(5a) Most food at restaurants, home, and schools is unhealthy (5b) Children cannot even identify raw vegetables
Part C	(8) We can solve the obesity problem with: (a) Corporate and government responsibility (b) Food education for families	(7) The Huntington Kitchen provides healthy food for 5,000 people for $25,000 a month
Conclusion	(9) If America solves its obesity epidemic, then the rest of the world will follow.	

TIP 41: Open with a question to get your audience thinking.

Asking a powerful question is the third reliable speech opening. For example, Jamie Oliver could have started out with "Why are 320 ordinary Americans just like you dying every day from the food they eat?"

If you want to go the powerful question route, I recommend that you use why questions and how questions. Questions that ask why are by far the most enticing since they tap into our natural curiosity to understand the world around us. Once we know why things happen, then we want to know how to make good things happen and how to prevent bad things from happening. If the why is implied or well understood, then you can open with a how question. Consider Mr. Oliver's message one more time. He could have led with "How can you prevent the food you eat from killing you?"

In the reformulated why and how openings I constructed for Jamie Oliver's speech, you probably noticed that I snuck in the word *you* a few times. That magical word transforms a good question into a great question by putting your listeners in introspective mode. You want them thinking about themselves and their world.

Simon Sinek[5] demonstrated the most effective powerful question opening of any TED Talk I have encountered. Here is how he began a talk that ultimately provided people with a how-to framework for being an inspiring leader or an effective corporation:

How do you explain when things don't go as we assume? Or better, how do you explain when others are able to achieve things that seem to defy all of the assumptions? For example: Why is Apple so innovative? Year after year, after year, after year, they're more innovative than all their competition. And yet, they're just a computer company. They're just like everyone else. They have the same access to the same talent, the same agencies, the same consultants, the same media. Then why is it that they seem to have something different? Why is it that Martin Luther King led the Civil Rights Movement? He wasn't the only man who suffered in a pre–civil rights America. And he certainly wasn't the only great orator of the day. Why him? And why is it that the Wright brothers were able to figure out control-powered, manned flight when there were certainly other teams who were better qualified, better funded, and they didn't achieve powered manned flight, and the Wright brothers beat them to it? There's something else at play here.

A single opening question is sufficient. But Mr. Sinek instead chose to bombard his audience with a string of why questions. This approach, an extended "why tease," is extremely effective but must be done carefully. In order to successfully string multiple questions together in an opening, all must have the same answer. I would just leave you confused if I opened a speech with "Why is the sky is blue? And why does a rolling stone gather no moss? And why are elephants afraid of mice?"

Simon also hooked the people in his audience by teasing them with the delights of secret knowledge:

> About three and a half years ago I made a discovery. And this discovery profoundly changed my view on how I thought the world worked, and it even profoundly changed the way in which I operate in it. As it turns out, there's a pattern. As it turns out, all the great and inspiring leaders and organizations in the world—whether it's Apple or Martin Luther King or the Wright brothers—they all think, act and communicate the exact same way. And it's the complete opposite to everyone else. All I did was codify it, and it's probably the world's simplest idea.

It is important to note that in addition to hooking his audience, Simon's introduction established the three-part architecture of his speech. The audience knew they would hear about Apple Computer, the Wright brothers, and Martin Luther King, Jr., and then they would be done.

Many speakers use the heavy-handed approach of telling their listeners what it is they are going to be told. Had Simon fallen into this trap, he would have said, "Today, I am going to tell you about Apple, the Wright brothers, and Martin Luther King. First, let's talk about Apple . . ." Boring! By hiding his plan inside his questions, Simon took a far more graceful approach that other speakers would be wise to learn.

TIP 42: Close your opening by giving the audience an explicit statement of benefits and a road map for the talk.

Your opening should cause your audience to consider the benefits of your talk in an implicit way. Close your opening by providing an explicit promise of the benefits that your audience will get and by noting how long it will take to get them.

For the longest time, I followed one of the three standard openings with a statement such as "In the next 45 minutes, I will share with you the three secrets to happiness." That is a pretty good statement of benefits. "I will share" is a lot better than "I will tell." However, it does have a couple of problems. First and foremost, it is speaker centric and not audience centric. The statement reveals what I am going to do, not what you are going to get. Second, it is not particularly sensory. A finisher to the opening should provide the audience with a visual metaphor of the structure of your speech. Applying these lessons, I would use the following: "Forty-five minutes from now, you will walk out of here with the three As of happiness in your toolbox." This statement is audience centric since it cues an audience to listen to my speech in order to pluck out the three As, along with an action-oriented visual.

Catchy mnemonics, such as acronyms or frameworks like the "three As," are a great way to provide the road map your listeners need. Resist the temptation to share what the acronym stands for at the beginning of your talk. The pleasure for the audience is in the progressive reveal over the course of your speech.

I have a strong preference for *three* because that is the stickiest number. You can have three steps, three themes, three strategies, three tips, three techniques, three tools. If you doubt this rule of thumb, consider the following. Everyone knows, thanks to Stephen Covey, that there are seven habits of highly effective people. Can you name them? There are 10 Commandments in the Bible, and the Bill of Rights of the U.S. Constitution comprises 10 amendments. Jack Welch preached the four Es of leadership. Can you name them? Thought so.

TIP 43: Steer clear of clichéd openings.

Since there is a limitless variety of ways you can open your speech, you should be aware of a few bad openings so that you do not commit the same sins as your forbearers. Of course, TED is selective about which videos it shares on TED.com. But what you may not be aware of is that it edits the chosen videos to remove verbal slips and anything that is awkward, insulting, or offensive. Consequently, it is impossible to find a terrible TED opening.

Nevertheless, there is plenty of badness out there from which to learn, so here is a quick list of what not to do:

- Do not open with a quote by a famous person you have never met—it is clichéd even if it is relevant.

- Do not open with a joke, for the same reason.

- Do not open with anything that could be even mildly offensive to your audience.

- Do not open with a Dilbert cartoon—oh, if I had a penny for every time I have seen this done . . .

- Do not open with "Thank you . . ."—if you want to thank your audience, do it at the end.

- Do not open with "Before I begin . . ."—since you just began.

TIP 44: Avoid audience participation openings unless the activity is critically relevant to your idea worth spreading.

There is another type of opening that is almost always a bad idea, and that is the activity opening. On the Internet, there is a fantastic speech posted to a video-sharing site on the topic of charismatic leadership. The content is highly valuable, and the presenter's delivery skills are impeccable. However, I took strong exception to his opening. To kick off his presentation, he asks the members of his audience to stand up, put their hand on their heart, turn around, and take one step forward. He then goes on to say that he can now report back to his own boss, when asked how the presentation went, that he "got them on their feet, touched their heart, turned them around, and got them moving in the right direction." It is a clever gimmick. But if you look closely at the audience members, many are displaying the body language of people who just realized they have been manipulated.

Every rule has its exceptions. If you have an activity that expresses your core message, engages the audience, and is fully genuine, then it can work. By way of example, in her TEDxFiDiWomen talk, Regena Thomashauer[6] has the core objective of inspiring women to embrace pleasure as a doorway to power, passion, enthusiasm, and creativity. Mama Gena is carried onto the stage by three men, with the sound of Pitbull's "I Know You Want Me" pulsing from the speakers. When the men set her down, she begins dancing and screams "Come on, dance with me!!!" As the camera pans back, you see that the people in the audience are instantly on their feet grooving to the beat. As the music dies down, she says:

> Wasn't that fun? Did you love that? Do you know what I was doing? I was flooding your body with nitric oxide! Do you know why? Because whenever we have a pleasurable experience, there are huge physical consequences. With just thirty seconds of fun, your blood starts to oxygenate and circulate. Nitric oxide is released and that turns on these neurotransmitters, including beta-endorphin and prolactin.

In this instance, there was 100 percent relevance between the activity—dancing—and the message. Mama Gena screams her passion and her purpose.

Once you finish your opening, you need to transition smoothly into the body of your speech. Transitioning is the subject of the next chapter.

CHAPTER 6

Transitioning Between Parts of Your Talk

TIP 45: Explicitly review the key point from your prior section and subtly preview the theme of your next section in your transition.

Imagine that you were to perfectly engineer a child from conception into an important novelist. You would start by joining two intellectuals, perhaps affiliated with a major university, in marriage. Then, if you got lucky, their offspring would start reading at a mere two years old. You would nourish her with the canon of Western literature from Shakespeare to Locke to Hemingway. Perhaps by age seven, she would start writing by building on the plots, settings, and characters of the stories she had fallen in love reading.

As she revealed in her TEDGlobal 2009 talk, this was the beginning of Nigerian author Chimamanda Adichie's[1] story. Table 6.1 provides a complete overview of her talk, which has the idea worth spreading: "to reject having a single story about groups of people so that we can better understand and embrace our individual diversity." Stated another way, her talk was a wake-up call to reject single stereotypes that dispossess people from positive individual and societal relationships. In her words, "The single story creates stereotypes, and the problem with stereotypes is not that they are untrue, but that they are incomplete. They make one story become the only story."

During her talk, Ms. Adichie took us from her youth reading classical Western literature, to discovering African authors, to her American university experiences, and finally on a trip to Mexico. Among the most impressive aspects of her speech is how she reviewed key points from the prior section and previewed the theme of her next section in her transitions. In an 18-minute TED Talk, each part may last as long as 5 minutes. In that case, you need to summarize the section with callbacks to the story you used or to the facts you revealed.

In Part A of her speech, Chimamanda reveals how she fell victim to the single story of how books should be written. Despite living in Nigeria, she wrote about white, blue-eyed characters who played in the snow and ate apples while she and her African friends played in the sun and ate mangoes. She transitioned into Part B with the following expert review and preview:

(Transition review) What this demonstrates, I think, is how impressionable and vulnerable we are in the face of a story, particularly as children. Because all I had read were books in which characters were foreign, I had become convinced that books, by their very nature, had to have foreigners in them, and had to be about things with which I could not personally identify. [Pause]

(Transition preview) Now, things changed when I discovered African books. There weren't many of them available. And they weren't quite as easy to find as the foreign books.

TABLE 6.1

Outline of Chimamanda Adichie's "The Danger of a Single Story" TED Talk

ELEMENT	PREMISE	PROOF
Introduction	(1) Preview theme: The danger of a single story	(2) I began reading British and American children's books at age two
Part A	(4) Children are impressionable and vulnerable to story	(3) At seven years old, I wrote in the style and point of view of the Western authors I read
Part B	(6) Reading stories by different kinds of authors saves you from having a single story of what books are	(5) Later, I discovered African authors who wrote about people I recognized
Part C	(8) Meeting other people saves you from having a single story of who they are	(7) I narrowly thought of my domestic helper as poor until I visited his village (9) My college roommate thought all Africans deserved pity based on Western literature dating back to 1561
Part D	(11) Single stories can be used to gain power by dispossessing people	(10) I had a single story of Mexicans as immigrants
Part E	(13) The problem with stereotypes is not that they are untrue, but that they are incomplete	(12) Stories of growing up with both happiness and strife
Conclusion	(15) "When we reject the single story, when we realize that there is never a single story about any place, we regain a kind of paradise"	(14a) What if I had more than one story about Mexico? (14b) What if my roommate had more than one story about Africa?

Notice that her transition review explicitly states the takeaway from the prior section of her talk—that people, and especially children, are vulnerable to the stories we consume. Because of limited attention spans, listeners fall into three categories: those who drifted in and out while you were speaking and have lost their place, those who were listening but have not had enough time to digest what you just said, and those lucky few who both heard and processed your message. Everyone will appreciate it if you summarize the point you were making.

Notice that her transition preview was as subtle as her transition review was explicit. Ms. Adichie gives her audience a sense that her writing would change with her exposure to African books. However, like any good storyteller, she gives her listeners just enough of a tease to pique their interest for the next part of her journey.

TIP 46: Provide clear verbal and visual cues that you are transitioning.

In this transition, Chimamanda Adichie recalls painting with a broad brush the stories and the facts that she had just shared about her experiences growing up reading British books. She paused before delivering her transition preview, "Now things changed . . ." Providing a pause of at least two or three seconds does a number of things for the members of your audience. First, it gives them time to grasp the explicit point of your last section. Second, listeners can fit that point into the overall logical agreement that you are making in your speech. Third, an extended pause is a clear and polished verbal signal that you are moving on to a new section. Fourth, and perhaps most important, listeners can use that silence to relate what you are saying to their own personal experiences.

Adichie delivered the transition in a more subdued conversational tone as compared with the more passionate tone she used in the main body sections. Her transition was subtle and smooth, while clearly signaling to the audience that she was going to show how African literature contrasted with British and American literature.

In addition to verbal cues, including pauses and shifts in tone, speakers can also employ visual cues signaling that they are about to transition. The best and most simple visual cue is to move to a different location on the stage. Ms. Adichie, like many other fiction writers who give TED Talks, was standing behind a lectern using notes, and this unfortunately limited her ability to use movement as a transition cue. For better and for worse, she did give a visual indication of shifting to her next section by looking down at her notes.

TIP 47: Orient your audience to where you are in your speech progression.

Imagine you are going to construct a building. You must first learn to lay a proper foundation before you build the walls and the roof. Your first building might be a bit sloppy, with clumsily exposed structural support columns. But you can rest assured that the building is going to stay standing. As you gain more experience, you learn to let form follow function. You learn to hide the structural elements when you want to hide them and expose them when you want them to stand out. You could follow the exposed "skin-and-bones" style of twentieth-century minimalist architect Ludwig Mies van der Rohe or apply the flowing, deconstructivist style of Guggenheim Bilbao architect Frank Gehry.

The journey of the speaker is much like the journey of the modern architect. One of the first things speakers learn about organization is building a foundation by creating the framework—which means that you tell your listeners what you are going to tell them, tell them, and then tell them again what you just told them. Novice speakers interpret this advice quite literally. They will give a speech that goes something like this:

(Opening) Why is it that some fruits heal your body and others make you fat? Ten minutes from now, you will walk out of this room with a grocery list of superfruits that are proven to add extra years to your life.

(Transition review) The three fruits are acai berries, goji berries, and pomegranates.

(Transition preview) Let's explore the health benefits of the first superfruit, acai berries . . .

Compared with speeches that lack structure, this is a very solid start. The people in the audience know exactly where the speaker is going, and they are primed to be convinced of why eating these three fruits can really result in a better and longer life. The problem, of course, is that the structural guts of the speech are too exposed. The key to advancing to the next level of speaking is to add a transition tease into your repertoire.

Consider the transition in the superfruit speech example above. Our imaginary speaker gave too much away by sharing the names of the three superfruits right off the bat. A better approach would have been to make a statement or to ask a question that gets listeners thinking about themselves while making them hungry for more information. For example: "What if you knew that three superfruits could give you 10 more years of active, healthy life? What if you knew that these fruits are easy to find and to add to a breakfast, lunch, or dinner menu?" These questions still prime the audience members to listen for the three items to add to their grocery list. It also teases them into remaining interested as each superfruit is revealed. Last, it opens the door for you to prove that the fruits really have the ability to keep them on the planet longer.

Great transitions explicitly review your prior section and subtly preview your next section. They also give your listeners precious moments to frame what you just shared in the context of your overall persuasive argument and to relate your talk to their personal experiences.

With openings and transitions squared away, the next chapter focuses on the critical skill of concluding your talk in a way that causes your audience to think, feel, and act differently as a result of hearing your idea worth spreading.

CHAPTER 7

Concluding Your Talk

TIP 48: Employ language that clearly signals you are concluding your talk.

Now it is time to draft your conclusion. When you provide a clear signal that you are moving to the conclusion of your speech, people will increase their level of attention. Thus, the language you use is critical. You can certainly get away with saying, "In conclusion . . ." However, you can do better. For example, you could also say, "We come to the end of our journey today and to the beginning of your future . . ." or "Now it is time for you to make a decision . . ."

Brené Brown,[1] a professor at the University of Houston College of Social Work, delivered one of the most powerful speech conclusions I have ever heard in a TED Talk. Her speech is outlined in Table 7.1. Dr. Brown's goal was to have people change their perspective on vulnerability from a source of pain to a source of power. She taught her audience to embrace vulnerability in order to live a fulfilled and a fulfilling life, and she reinforced that message in her conclusion by saying:

> *But there's another way, and I leave you with this. This is what I have found: to let ourselves be seen, deeply seen, vulnerably seen;*

TABLE 7.1

Outline of Brené Brown's "The Power of Vulnerability" TED Talk

ELEMENT	PREMISE	PROOF
Introduction	(1a) *Prologue.* Story about convincing an emcee at a prior engagement to refer to her as a "researcher storyteller" (1b) Introduce theme in general as "expanding perception"	
Part A	(3) Connection gives purpose and meaning to our lives	(2) My research showed that shame unravels connection
Part B	(5) Connect to yourself by having the courage to embrace vulnerability	(4) My research found that people who felt loved were the ones who felt worthy of being loved
Part C	(7) You cannot selectively numb emotions; joy and struggle are a package deal	(6) I enlisted a therapist in my fight to be able to embrace my own vulnerability
Conclusion	(8) By accepting your vulnerability, you will be kinder to yourself and to others	

to love with our whole hearts, even though there's no guarantee and that's really hard, and I can tell you as a parent, that's excruciatingly difficult to practice gratitude and joy in those moments of terror, when we're wondering, "Can I love you this much? Can I believe in this this passionately? Can I be this fierce about this?" just to be able to stop and, instead of catastrophizing what might happen, to say, "I'm just so grateful, because to feel this vulnerable means I'm alive." And the last, which I think is probably the most important, is to believe that we're enough. Because when we work from a place I believe that says, "I'm enough," then we stop screaming and start listening, we're kinder and gentler to the people around us, and we're kinder and gentler to ourselves.

That's all I have. Thank you.

Notice that Dr. Brown used not one but three transitional phrases to signal that she was moving into her conclusion: "But there's another way," "I leave you with this," and "This is what I have found." Delivery of these phrases was separated with an attention-grabbing pause.

Here are examples of how 10 popular TED speakers signaled the move into the conclusion of their talk. As you read them, notice how they each adopt one or more of the following patterns: final thought or example, takeaway, call to action, and brighter future.

- Benjamin Zander: "So now, I have one last thought, which is that it really makes a difference what we say—the words that come out of our mouth . . ."[2]

- Bunker Roy: "I'll just wind up by saying that I think you don't have to look for solutions outside . . ."[3]

- Cameron Russell: "If there's a takeaway to this talk, I hope it's that we all feel more comfortable acknowledging the power of image in our perceived successes and our perceived failures."[4]

- Deb Roy: "So I want to leave you with one last memorable moment from our family. This is the first time our son took more than two steps at once—captured on film . . ." [5]

- Jamie Oliver: "And look, I know it's weird having an English person standing here before you talking about all this. All I can say is: I care. I'm a father, and I love this country, and I believe truly, actually, that if change can be made in this country, beautiful things will happen around the world . . ."[6]

- Jill Bolte Taylor: "So who are we? We are the life-force power of the universe, with manual dexterity and two cognitive minds. And we have the power to choose, moment by moment, who and how we want to be in the world . . ."[7]

- Richard St. John: "So, the big—the answer to this question is simple . . ."[8]

- Rory Sutherland: "Two quotations to more or less end with. One of them is . . ."[9]

- Salman Khan: "Now imagine what happens where . . ."[10]

- Susan Cain: "And so I am going to leave you now with three calls for action for those who share this vision . . ."[11]

One way to effectively signal a conclusion is to shorten your sentences and add passion to your voice. Switch from using *I* to saying *you* or *we, us, our*. The enemy of the good is the great, so I am wary of messing with the near perfection of Dr. Brown's talk. If I were to make one change, it would be to replace her *I*-centric language with the singular *you*.

TIP 49: Explicitly summarize your idea worth spreading in your conclusion.

Karen Thompson Walker[12] released her debut novel, *The Age of Miracles,* on the same day that she delivered her talk at TEDGlobal. The book, told from the perspective of a preteen girl, is a coming-of-age tale set against the backdrop of the end of the world. Thematically, it asks whether hope and love can prevail in the face of cataclysmic uncertainty. While her book tackled the fictional implications of ambiguity, her TED Talk addressed the practical considerations of assessing risk in order to make better decisions. Her idea worth spreading, outlined in Table 7.2, is "to see fear as a gift rather than a weakness so that we can see accurately into the future."

Writers, particularly fiction writers, are among the most effective speakers to grace the TED stage. Ms. Walker wove her logical treatise on embracing fear with a nearly 200-year-old story of a shipwreck

TABLE 7.2

Outline of Karen Thompson Walker's "What Fear Can Teach Us" TED Talk

ELEMENT	PREMISE	PROOF
Introduction	(2) We know what it is like to be afraid, but we do not spend enough time thinking about what our fears mean	(1) In 1819, 20 sailors huddled in three lifeboats after their whaling ship sank
Part A	(4) What if we thought of fear as an amazing act of imagination rather than a weakness to be overcome?	(3) I grew up in California fearing killer earthquakes and monsters under my bed
Part B	(6) Fears are stories we tell ourselves that help us prepare for the future	(5) The 20 sailors needed to choose between three increasingly distant destinations fraught with cannibals, storms, or starvation
Part C	(8) To make effective decisions in the face of fear, we must temper our vivid artistic ability with cool scientific judgment	(7) The sailors chose the longest journey, but half of them died of starvation
Conclusion	(9) Our fears are an amazing gift of the imagination that can give us literature and truth	

that was the basis of Herman Melville's *Moby-Dick*. Through to her conclusion, her talk sets out the following deductive premise chain: we do not spend enough time thinking about what our fears mean; if we did, then we would see them as a gift of imagination rather than a weakness; this gift allows us to peer into our future; but we must marry our vivid imagination with scientific judgment in order to make effective decisions. She explicitly pulls her entire argument together in her powerful conclusion as an inspiring, audience-centric message:

And maybe if we all tried to read our fears, we too would be less often swayed by the most salacious among them. Maybe then we'd spend less time worrying about serial killers and plane crashes and more time concerned with the subtler and slower disasters we face: the silent buildup of plaque in our arteries, the gradual changes in our climate. Just as the most nuanced stories in literature are often the richest, so too might our subtlest fears be the truest. Read in the right way, our fears are an amazing gift of the imagination, a kind of everyday clairvoyance, a way of glimpsing what might be the future when there's still time to influence how that future will play out. Properly read, our fears can offer us something as precious as our favorite works of literature: a little wisdom, a bit of insight and a version of that most elusive thing—the truth. Thank you.

Notice that Karen Thompson Walker's conclusion is not a bland book report–style summary. With the exception of the sentence about serial killers, plane crashes, and arterial plaque buildup, she also wisely avoided the temptation to introduce new material at the end. Finally, by starting with "And maybe if we all tried to read our fears," she delivered a smooth callback to her introduction that ended with "I'm not sure we spend enough time thinking about what our fears mean."

TIP 50: Finish with an audience-centric call to action that is urgent and easy to execute.

When you build a case for change in your speech, the conclusion is your final opportunity to inspire your listeners and alter their perspective or to call them to action. To do this, you must create a sense of urgency. Since change is hard, provide the people in your audience with an easy next step they can take today to get moving in a positive direction. If warranted, you might play the fear card by including, "The consequences of failure are . . ."

Brené Brown's conclusion is brilliant. It is powerful, personal, and emotional. Her questions raise the tension level of the audience by touching the third rail of self-doubt. Then she immediately provides a salve of inspiring affirmation: "I'm enough." When you are feeling vulnerable, respond by saying, "I'm enough." That is her simple-as-can-be call to action that every audience member can apply immediately.

Karen Thompson Walker's "What Fear Can Teach Us" offers a similarly empowering personal response to an emotion usually perceived as negative. Once again, listeners can easily and instantly apply this advice to improve their level of self-satisfaction.

TIP 51: End with a "thank you."

One final thought on closing out your speech. You might have noticed that both Brené Brown and Karen Walker Thompson ended their talk with a "thank you." An eternal debate rages about whether or not these should be the last words out of your mouth. In the yes camp, supporters say it is a final act of gratitude to cement your bond with the audience. In the no camp, detractors retort that it steals from your central message and may open a little crack in your armor of confidence. They are both right, and there really is no correct answer. What I can tell you is that almost all TED speakers end their speech with a thank you, and so you cannot go wrong following this unwritten rule. An acceptable alternative is how Nigel Marsh ended his talk on achieving a work-life balance: "And that, I think, is an idea worth spreading."

You have been exposed to all the best practices and lessons learned from the best TED speakers and have everything you need to develop the content for your idea worth spreading.

Before proceeding to how to deliver your TED Talk, I need to share an important consideration. Though not grounded in statistically rigorous research, I firmly believe that content is king. Your goal should be to become an expert who speaks rather than an expert speaker. Experts who speak focus principally on content; expert speakers spend the majority of the time perfecting delivery. As a philosophical principle, your delivery just needs to be "good enough" to be consistent with your content and not otherwise distracting. Too much or too little polish will distract you from your audience. Case in point is that almost all the most popular and impactful TED Talks are delivered by people who think and write for a living. I was not surprised to discover that many are by admission introverted and terribly afraid of speaking in public.

But what about the studies from Mehrabian, Ferris, and Wiener in 1967 that showed communication is 7 percent content, 38 percent vocal tone, and 55 percent body language? Tragically, those studies continue to be misinterpreted. In fact, the studies were designed to estimate the impact those three factors had on how listeners assessed their feelings toward a speaker as liking, neutrality, and disliking. Dr. Mehrabian later wrote, "Unless a communicator is talking about their feelings or attitudes, these equations are not applicable." The correct takeaway from the study is that your delivery should be in harmony with your content. And that is the idea worth spreading that we will focus on in the next part of this book.

PART II

DELIVERY

CHAPTER 8

Projecting Emotion

TIP 52: Bring your audience through the broadest possible emotional range.

The most memorable speakers bring their audiences through the broadest possible emotional range. However, few novice speakers have ever taken the time to define what that range actually is. If you vaguely strive to connect on an emotional level, you are just as likely to hit as miss the mark.

Classifying emotion is not a trivial exercise. Two distinguished researchers, Paul Ekman and Robert Plutchik, have espoused overlapping but not identical theories. By studying facial microexpressions across cultures, Ekman identified six primary emotions: anger, disgust, fear, happiness, sadness, and surprise. Plutchik, in his visually memorable Wheel of Emotions, posited eight paired emotions: joy-sadness, trust-disgust, fear-anger, and surprise-anticipation.

Though either system will suit you quite well, I have found that a hybrid of the two is most effective for speech development. My "six emotions for speaking" include anger, disgust, fear, happiness, love, and sadness. I eliminated surprise since it is so fleeting and quickly morphs into one of the other emotions as people process the impact of what surprised them; ditto for anticipation. Last, I transformed trust into love because love is a more powerful and more commonly elicited emotion in public speaking. (The Wheel of Emotions treats love as a composite of joy and trust, but we have all seen love exist without either.)

Let's look at how punk musician Amanda Palmer[1] touched on each of these emotions in her TED Talk outlined in Table 8.1. Her idea worth spreading is "to give freely and ask for help freely so that art is restored in the fabric of our communities."

- *Anger.* "And I would get harassed sometimes. People would yell at me from their passing cars. 'Get a job!' "

- *Disgust.* "I love telling people I did this [being a living statue street performer] for a job, because everybody always wants to know, who are these freaks in real life?"

- *Fear.* "I tweeted for a crash pad, and at midnight, I'm ringing a doorbell on the Lower East Side, and it occurs to me I've never actually done this alone. I've always been with my band or my crew. Is this what stupid people do? Is this how stupid people die?"

- *Happiness.* "And meanwhile, my band is becoming bigger and bigger. We signed with a major label."

- *Love.* "I maintain couch-surfing and crowd-surfing are basically the same thing. You're falling into the audience and you're trusting each other."

- *Sadness.* "So I had the most profound encounters with people, especially lonely people who looked like they hadn't talked to anyone in weeks . . ."

TIP 53: Invite your audience to "imagine."

One of the most powerful ways to inspire your audience is to kindle deep introspection. The more concretely listeners visualize

TABLE 8.1

Outline of Amanda Palmer's "The Art of Asking" TED Talk

ELEMENT	PREMISE	PROOF
Introduction	(2) Being a street performer allowed me to connect with people, get a practical education, and earn a living wage	(1) "Five years after graduating from college, I was a living statue called the 8-foot bride"
Part A	(4) I continued to make an art out of asking people for help to maintain a human connection	(3) Eventually, I quit and started touring full-time with the Dresden Dolls
Part B	(6) Strangers are more generous and trustworthy than you would assume	(5) Twitter came along and made it easy to ask for anything, anywhere
Part C	(8) It is better to ask people to pay for art and trust them than to make them pay	(7) A major record label signed us then dropped us after "only" selling 25,000 albums. So we decided to give our music away for free in exchange for voluntary donations
Conclusion	(9) Though technology is helping artists restore their connection with the community, it is more important to face one another and share without shame in order to help one another	

their own participation in your story or with your ideas, the more likely they are to take the actions required to change their world. Fortunately, there is one magical word—*imagine*—that triggers the brain to instantly visualize almost anything.

In her TEDIndia 2009 talk, Jane Chen[2] shared a concept for a low-cost, lifesaving incubator with the potential to save the lives of millions of premature babies in the developing world. She began her talk as follows:

> *Please close your eyes and open your hands. Now imagine what*
> *you could place in your hands: an apple, maybe your wallet. Now*
> *open your eyes. What about a life?*

As she asked "What about a life?" Ms. Chen revealed an Anne Geddes image of a tiny baby sleeping in the palm of a pair of aged hands. In this instance, the question was abstract enough that the image added specificity and emotional intensity. Most of the time, it is best to just let people's imaginations run wild. The freedom of imagination explains why the book is always better than the movie.

Jane Chen used the word *imagine* to enhance an activity that her audience completed in the room. However, an even more powerful approach is to use this magical word to invite your audience to be a fly on the wall in your stories. For example, you might start out by saying, "Imagine you were with me the day I met my wife . . ."

After you ask the people in your audience to imagine, you must then give them a nice long pause so they can create a visual image or scan their brain for a suitable memory. That requires a much longer silence than many speakers are comfortable with—at least 3 to 5 seconds.

Amateur speakers focus only on the visual. When professional speakers ask their audience to imagine, they strive to engage all five senses—sight, smell, touch, taste, and sound. For example: "Imagine you were with me the first time I visited New York City. Coming from a small midwestern town, I was certain that I was surrounded by muggers at every turn. Have you ever felt there was danger at every turn? On that sweltering August day, I choked on the smell of taxicab exhaust mixed with the sweat of pedestrians pressed shoulder to shoulder on every street . . ."

The word *imagine* is just as powerful at the end of your speech as it is at the beginning. In your conclusion, ask people to picture their lives if they applied your inspirational message. "Imagine what your life would be like if you woke up tomorrow with compassion for your friends. Imagine what your life would be like if you woke up tomorrow with compassion for your family. Imagine what your life would be like if you woke up tomorrow with compassion for . . . yourself."

The word *imagine* can be used either to bring your listeners into your stories or to prompt them to visualize their past or their future. When bringing people into your stories, you need to provide a very high level of detail that engages all five senses. However, if you are trying to get the members of your audience to think about themselves, then back off on supplying detail to allow them the freedom to explore their thoughts.

The next time you speak, ask your audience to imagine at least twice. At the beginning of your speech, do this by drawing individuals into a vivid, sensory story. At the end, the technique is to invite your listeners to imagine their future if they apply your message. Imagine how much more inspiring your speech will be . . .

TIP 54: Be vulnerable and express your emotions, but don't lose control.

There is an unwritten and unspoken rule that says that as we mature into adult professionals, we need to become perfect robots, devoid of outward emotional expression. However, when we are with the people we love, we allow our torrent of positive and negative emotions to flow more freely. This openness is the basis for the deep connections that sustain us.

The speakers who leave the deepest and longest-lasting impressions on their listeners treat them as close friends. They take themselves to the limit of emotional control by reliving their most joyful and most vulnerable moments on stage. Amanda Palmer does an excellent job of this; however, Jill Bolte Taylor[3] serves as the better example. As she delivered her final words, her voice began to crack and tears began to flow. With the audience members on their feet, organizer Chris Anderson walked over to give Ms. Taylor a warm hug. She gave everything she had in order to share her idea worth spreading.

These two examples are of female speakers operating at their emotional edge—does that mean that this rule does not also apply to men? Due to cultural norms, males need to work even harder to disclose emotions that connect them with their audience.

On January 15, 2009, US Airways Flight 1549, with its 155 occupants, lost both engines to a flock of Canada geese less than three minutes into its climb out of New York City's LaGuardia Airport. Though the story had a happy ending when the cool-thinking flight crew opted to land in the Hudson River, the flight was six minutes of pure terror for everyone on board. Having survived the plane crash, Ric Elias[4] got his chance to deliver his TED Talk, outlined in Table 8.2, just over two years later. He elicited emotion when talking about his family:

> And that sadness really framed [it all] in one thought, which was, I only wish for one thing. I only wish I could see my kids grow up.

When he delivered those lines, his voice was softer and his speech slower as he paused to collect his emotions so that he could continue speaking. This was a genuine and not manufactured emotion that became the defining moment in his talk. It was when he forged a true bond that allowed the audience to accept his idea worth spreading.

The next chapter delves into the creative use of language for inspiration.

TABLE 8.2

Outline of Ric Elias's "3 Things I Learned While My Plane Crashed" TED Talk

ELEMENT	PREMISE	PROOF
Introduction	(1) Three things ran through my head when the plane I was on lost both engines and the pilot said, "Brace for impact"	
Part A	(3) Life can change in an instant, so do not postpone anything	(2) "If the wine is ready and the person is there, I'm opening it"
Part B	(5) Eliminate negative energy from your life	(4) I let my ego grow, and I wasted time on the wrong people
Part C	(7) My only goal in life is to be a great father	(6) The prospect of dying was not scary, it was sad
Conclusion	(8) Don't wait for your plane to crash to improve your relationships and to be the best parent you can be	

CHAPTER 9

Enhancing Your Language

TIP 55: Polish your speech with rhetorical wordplay.

In her TED Talk, Harvard Business School professor Amy Cuddy[1] shared an idea that was both incredibly easy and incredibly valuable: "to spend two minutes power posing before going into stressful situations so that you can achieve better outcomes." The outline of her talk is provided in Table 9.1.

She also employed a vast array of rhetorical devices to enhance her speech. Though some have unfamiliar names, you will recognize most of them from the examples provided:

- *Assonance and consonance.* These kissing cousins refer to the repetition of the same sound two or more times in rapid succession. Assonance is the repetition of vowel sounds; consonance is the repetition of consonant sounds. Ms. Cuddy's consonance "power posing" is much more memorable than "stand big and tall with your head high and your arms outstretched."

TABLE 9.1

Outline of Amy Cuddy's "Your Body Language Shapes Who You Are" TED Talk

ELEMENT	PREMISE	PROOF
Prologue	(1) I am going to offer you a free, no-tech, two-minute life hack that could significantly change the way your life unfolds	
Introduction	(3) We are familiar with the fact that we judge others and are judged by others based on body language	(2) Examples of politicians with noticeable nonverbal gaffes
Part A	(5) Nonverbal power dynamics are partly responsible for the gender performance gap in schools	(4) Animals express power and dominance by opening up and becoming big
Part B	(6) Our minds change our bodies	(7) When alpha primates take over, their testosterone levels go up and their cortisol (stress) levels go down
Part C	(8) Our bodies change our minds	(9) People who assumed power poses for two minutes show increased risk tolerance and 25% lower cortisol levels
Conclusion	(10) Fake it till you make it—spend two minutes power posing before going into stressful situations so that you can achieve better outcomes	

- *Anaphora, epistrophe, and symploce.* As noted in an earlier chapter, anaphora is the repetition of the same word or words at the beginning of successive phrases or sentences. Epistrophe is the same concept applied to the ends of phrases or sentences. Symploce combines the two. Amy used symploce in the following pair of sentences: "*We* don't *want* to prime *them* with a concept of *power. We want them* to be feeling *power.*"

- *Anadiplosis.* This is the repetition of the last word of one sentence at or near the beginning of the next. Professor Cuddy used this technique when she posed the question, "We know that our minds change our bodies, but is it also true that our bodies change our minds?"

- *Hendiatris.* This is the use of three words or phrases in succession to express a single concept. At the beginning of her speech, Ms. Cuddy posed a question and then answered with a succession of three fungible examples: "So how many of you are sort of making yourselves smaller? Maybe you're hunching, crossing your legs, maybe wrapping your ankles."

In addition to these fancier rhetorical techniques, the good old rhyming of words and repetition of phrases or sentences are powerful ways to underscore key messages.

TIP 56: Apply the rule of three in lists of similar items.

In 1956, Princeton psychologist George A. Miller published a groundbreaking article entitled "The Magical Number Seven, Plus or Minus Two: Some Limits on Our Capacity for Processing Information." In it, he summarized experiments that tested how accurately people were able to first absorb and then communicate different amounts of information.

Over the years, many academics have tested the validity of what has come to be known as Miller's law: the idea that people can hold seven, plus or minus two, items in their working memory. Though the magical number seven remains embedded in conventional wisdom, scientists agree that there is no single magical number. The number of items we are able to remember depends on the size of each information chunk, the relationship between the chunks, and our individual cognitive ability.

However, with the advent of modern brain imaging, three scholars rose to Miller's challenge to discover if there really is a magical number. Jennifer J. Summerfield, Demis Hassabis, and Eleanor A. Maguire asked 19 people to construct imaginary scenes in their minds as they listened to groups of short phrases. Each phrase contained a descriptor and a noun. For example, one group of three phrases was "a dark blue carpet," "a carved chest of drawers," and "an orange striped pencil." They tested groups of three to six elements while they watched the brain activity of the subjects using functional magnetic resonance imaging technology. In addition, they asked the people to indicate on a keypad how difficult they found the trial, the vividness of the imagined scene, and the perceived degree of integration between the elements.

The researchers made two important discoveries. First, brain activity steadily increased in the core locations of the brain up to and including the addition of a third element. Then, activity suddenly stabilized. Second, subjects rated the tests with three elements as easiest to visualize, most vivid, and most integrated.

If you are wondering what all this has to do with public speaking, it is that the types of lists Summerfield, Hassabis, and Maguire studied are *exactly* the kinds of lists that speakers use. There is something satisfying and symmetrical about the rule of three.

TIP 57: Ask questions to engage listeners in conversation.

During the course of each section, you should frequently ask your listeners questions that get them reflecting on their own lives. This technique transforms a speech into a conversation. Audience members are still able to reply in their minds and with their body language. In smaller forums, you can actually solicit verbal responses.

In her 20.6-minute talk (yes, she went over time, but no one seemed to mind), Amy Cuddy asked 40 questions, or nearly 2 per minute. For those keeping score, speakers who delivered the most popular TED

Talks typically ranged from 0 to 2 questions per minute, with an average just over 1. Hence, Professor Cuddy was on the upper end.

Some speakers intentionally ask questions that stump their audience. Questions in this category often start with something like, "What do you think is the secret to . . .?" The speaker's hope is that the listeners will get the answer wrong either out loud or in their heads. Being wrong is a strong motivator for wanting to listen to hear the truth. Though the psychological basis is accurate and does work, I do not recommend this technique because it is not a compassionate speaking practice. Your audience may experience negative emotions during your talk, but those emotions should be a natural rather than manufactured reaction.

The good news is that there are better ways to use questions that engage. Amy Cuddy demonstrated all four of them:

- *Polling.* "So how many of you are sort of making yourselves smaller?"

- *Seeking confirmation (aka adding question tags).* "If you use [emoticons] poorly [in online negotiations], bad idea, right?"

- *Provoking thought.* "Can power posing for a few minutes really change your life in meaningful ways?"

- *Creating suspense.* "So I'm watching this behavior in the classroom, and what do I notice?"

The first two cases, polling and seeking confirmation, are closed-ended questions that have no wrong answer. The final two, provoking thought and creating suspense, are intended to stimulate the audience to either apply the talk to their own lives or invoke their imaginations.

One final consideration is to pause and nod to acknowledge your audience's unspoken thoughts after you ask a question. This will sustain a two-way dialogue even though your audience cannot respond verbally.

TIP 58: Interpret statistics to make them individually emotionally relevant.

Remember to interpret all statistics, particularly large numbers, with vivid, emotional, personally relevant analogies or metaphors. I find it most valuable to start with a general statistic and then make it personal. For example, the combination of the following pair of sentences is stronger than if either were delivered alone: "Seventy million Americans live with heart disease every day. Odds are that you or one of the three people sitting next to you will die from heart disease."

Interpreting statistics with more granular statistics is not the only way to make abstract numbers concrete. Amy Cuddy's world as a social scientist is filled with impenetrable statistics; however, consider how she deftly translates dry hormone percentage changes into emotional language:

> Here's what we find on testosterone . . . high-power people experience about a 20-percent increase, and low-power people experience about a 10-percent decrease. Here's what you get on cortisol. High-power people experience about a 25-percent decrease, and the low-power people experience about a 15-percent increase. So two minutes lead to these hormonal changes that configure your brain to basically either be assertive, confident and comfortable, or really stress-reactive, and, you know, feeling sort of shut down.

TIP 59: Intensify your language with vivid images and sensory detail.

Your verbal delivery extends beyond speech mechanics into the words that you use. To enhance your audience's interest, make liberal use of vivid, descriptive, sensory detail. Sights, sounds, and smells are the easiest to incorporate. In some situations, you may even be able to weave in taste and touch. The small penalty you pay in being verbose is more than made up for by the impact you have of allowing your audience to form a mental picture. During her conclusion, Amy Cuddy was visually prescriptive in where to apply her power-posing idea worth spreading:

> *Tiny tweaks can lead to big changes. So this is two minutes. Two minutes, two minutes, two minutes. Before you go into the next stressful evaluative situation, for two minutes, try doing this, in the elevator, in a bathroom stall, at your desk behind closed doors.*

TIP 60: Use the pronouns *I, you,* and *we* as you would in one-on-one conversation.

In his 1936 classic *How to Win Friends and Influence People*, Dale Carnegie said, "Remember that a person's name is to that person the sweetest and most important sound in any language." When I first read Carnegie's book, I was quite taken with this advice and thought hard about how to apply it when presenting to large audiences. Since addressing people by name is not practical in groups larger than 10, I figured that I could get very close to my audience by using the word *you* in the singular as frequently as possible.

However, this technique was not without its problems. If you have ever spoken to a salesperson who used your name over and over, it begins to feel superficial and patronizing after a certain point. The same is true of motivational speakers who constantly tell you what you must do. The simple solution is using pronouns as you would in normal one-on-one conversation. For instance, use *I* when you are telling personal stories or expressing your opinion and use *you* when you are asking questions or issuing a call to action.

By way of example, consider TED speaker Ric Elias. He used the pronouns *I* and *my* more than 14 times per minute. This is double the average of 7 per minute for most TED Talks but typical for speeches that are personal stories. For the majority of his talk, Mr. Elias recounted his inner dialogue in the first person as the airplane he was on went down:

> *I'm saying, "Please blow up." I don't want this thing to break in 20 pieces like you've seen in those documentaries. And as we're coming down, I had a sense of, wow, dying is not scary. It's almost like we've been preparing for it our whole lives. But it was very sad. I didn't want to go; I love my life.*

In the last lines of his speech, Mr. Elias switched from *I* to *you* in order to explicitly share the moral of his story:

> *How would you change? What would you get done that you're waiting to get done because you think you'll be here forever? How would you change your relationships and the negative energy in them? And more than anything, are you being the best parent you can?*

For those keeping score, Mr. Elias used *you* or *your* with a frequency of four times per minute. That is typical of the average TED Talk. Again, as you construct your talk, you should not count your use of pronouns; there is no golden ratio that applies to every kind of talk, let alone one kind. Instead, simply be intentional about the point of view from which you tell stories, share information, and issue calls to action.

Your goal is to engage your audience as individuals. To that end, beware of using forms of *you* in the plural such as the phrases *you all, every one of you, all of you,* or *some of you.* The same applies to words that envelop you and your entire audience such as *we* and *us.* Instead of asking "How many of you have . . . ," ask "Have you . . ." or "Raise your hand if you have . . ."

TIP 61: Use the smallest and simplest words to express your message.

There is a myth that great speakers need to use extensive vocabularies. A speaker's job is to connect emotionally with her listeners and inspire them to look at the world differently. A speaker's job is not to impress an audience with vocabulary. If you tax the audience's cognitive processing ability, then you will fail to connect. Speeches should be written for the ear and not for the eye.

Devised by Rudolf Flesch and developed by J. Peter Kincaid, the Flesch-Kincaid (F-K) grade-level algorithm was first used in 1978 to measure the difficulty of technical manuals used by the U.S. military. Today, it forms the basis of the readability statistics in Microsoft Word.

As it turns out, Amy Cuddy was right on target with using the smallest and simplest possible words to express her message. On the F-K scale, popular TED Talks ranged at grade levels between 3.7 and 9.6. At 6.1, Amy was just shy of the average of 6.6.

Contrary to what you might assume, the F-K score is not based on a dictionary. It does not know that *genre, chord structures*, and *improvisation* are more complex than *type, harmony,* and *creativity.* The grade level goes up for two simple reasons. The first reason it increases is due to long sentences. The second is when the text contains a great number of multisyllabic words. Just remember, listeners like short sentences punctuated by pauses.

When speakers take the stage and transform themselves into their ultrapoised alter egos, rather than appearing more professional and intelligent, they often achieve the opposite and cause their audience to disconnect from them. The tips in this chapter are intended to remind you to choose the same words for onstage delivery as you would in natural conversation.

Perhaps the biggest error that novice speakers commit is equating professionalism with gravity and solemnity. This misguided idea leads people to scrub the humor, which is present in their everyday interactions with others, out of their speeches. The next chapter shows you how to make effective use of humor.

CHAPTER 10

Adding Humor

TIP 62: Crank up the laughs per minute with humor based on a sense of superiority.

In order to understand how to effectively add humor to your talk, we must first delve into the psychology of laughter. At present, there is no grand unified theory of why people laugh. There are three theories of why humans laugh that are complementary and overlapping. The first theory is to claim superiority. A great deal of humor falls squarely into this category, including laughing at people who make bad decisions or are eccentric. This type of humor is amplified when people are in a position of authority and when they fit particular stereotypes—some politically correct and some not. Humor based on superiority has an escalating scale of viciousness starting with gentle parody and satire, moving to moderate sarcasm, and progressing to scathing insults.

With fair warning that deconstructing humor destroys it, consider how social scientist Hans Rosling,[1] in his 2007 TED Talk on global economic development, took aim at the academic elite:

> *But one late night, when I was compiling the report, I really realized my discovery. I have shown that Swedish top students know*

statistically significantly less about the world than chimpanzees . . .
I did also an unethical study of the professors of the Karolinska
Institute—that hands out the Nobel Prize in Medicine, and they
are on par with the chimpanzee.

We love to bring authority down a few notches since it gives us a sense of superiority. This, of course, can result in some very cruel and offensive humor of which you should steer clear in your TED Talk, not to mention in your life. However, there are some constituencies that are still politically correct to make fun of, namely academics and politicians.

TIP 63: Crank up the laughs per minute with the element of surprise.

The second theory of why humans laugh is the element of surprise. We human beings delight in experiencing turns of events that challenge our expectations and our sensibilities. For example, consider the following joke attributed to Joe Pasquale: "See this, it's my step ladder. My real one left when I was three." Or better still, at least if you are a math nerd or know one, reflect upon this joke of unknown origin: "An independent variable is one that does not need other variables to feel good about itself." In both these examples, the humor comes from the unexpected twist that challenges what you were expecting to hear.

A short list of the types of humor accounted for by this theory includes sheer absurdity, bad advice, exaggeration or farce, irony, puns or plays on words, screwball comedy, physical comedy, and the cousins overstatement and understatement. People are delightfully surprised by witty incongruity or shock.

Exaggerated reality, too, is always good for a laugh. The simple way to express humor through exaggerated reality is to put a normal person in an extraordinary situation or an extraordinary person in a normal situation. Some examples of this are nonchalantly ignoring extreme danger, reacting excessively to minor offenses, and relentlessly pursuing futility. For example, Sir Ken Robinson,[2] the most viewed TED speaker to date, puts an extraordinary person—Shakespeare—in an ordinary situation:

> Because you don't think of Shakespeare being a child, do you?
> Shakespeare being seven? I never thought of it. I mean, he was
> seven at some point. He was in somebody's English class, wasn't
> he? How annoying would that be? "Must try harder." Being sent
> to bed by his dad, you know, to Shakespeare, "Go to bed, now," to
> William Shakespeare, "and put the pencil down. And stop speak-
> ing like that. It's confusing everybody."

TIP 64: Crank up the laughs per minute with emotional release or catharsis.

The third theory is that people laugh to release strong emotions. Often, laughter is a salve to the darker emotions of embarrassment and fear. Morbid humor, also known as gallows humor, is explained well by this theory; we laugh to dismiss fears of our own mortality. Similarly, laughing at scatological or sexual humor discharges embarrassment. (Yes, though admittedly juvenile, the pun was definitely intended in the prior sentence.)

Recall Ric Elias[3] who survived the "miracle on the Hudson" plane crash. Despite his dark subject matter, Mr. Elias delivered just over one laugh per minute. As you can see in his introduction, most of these relied on emotional release:

> Imagine a big explosion as you climb through 3,000 ft. Imagine a
> plane full of smoke. Imagine an engine going clack, clack, clack,
> clack, clack, clack, clack. It sounds scary. Well I had a unique seat
> that day. I was sitting in 1D. I was the only one who could talk to

the flight attendants. So I looked at them right away, and they said, "No problem. We probably hit some birds." The pilot had already turned the plane around, and we weren't that far. You could see Manhattan. Two minutes later, three things happened at the same time. The pilot lines up the plane with the Hudson River. That's usually not the route. [Laughter] He turns off the engines. Now imagine being in a plane with no sound. And then he says three words—the most unemotional three words I've ever heard. He says, "Brace for impact." I didn't have to talk to the flight attendant anymore. [Laughter] I could see in her eyes, it was terror. Life was over.

TIP 65: Use self-deprecating humor that works on multiple levels.

Together, these three theories—superiority, surprise, and release—encompass nearly every type of humor. But you should think of them as three partially overlapping circles in a Venn diagram. Though most jokes are best explained by one theory, it is clear that many work on two of these levels and some on all three. Self-deprecating humor always hits on at least two. First, this type of humor allows others to feel superior at the speaker's expense. Second, audiences expect speakers to be competent and confident. Consequently, when a speaker makes a self-deprecating remark, the audience gets a delightful surprise and responds with laugher. Often that laughter is rooted in empathy. Certain types of self-deprecating humor even include the emotional release theory, too—for example, when the speaker makes light of his own illness.

Self-deprecating humor is particularly easy and effective. As a society, we are conditioned to keep up appearances. We laugh with automatic delight when speakers let their guard down and reveal that they are, in fact, flawed human beings. We laugh when others reveal their bad judgment. We even laugh when they share stories of physical pain, as long as they managed to escape relatively unscathed—although Mel Brooks might disagree with this latter half of the statement: "[From your perspective] tragedy is when you break a nail, comedy is when I fall through an open manhole and die."

In her 2008 TED Talk, brain researcher Jill Bolte Taylor[4] described how she studied her own stroke as it happened. This topic could bring people to tears. And yet Ms. Taylor had her audience rolling on the floor laughing by revealing to them what a supernerd she is:

> And in that moment, my right arm went totally paralyzed by my side. Then I realized, "Oh my gosh! I'm having a stroke! I'm having a stroke!" And the next thing my brain says to me is, "Wow! This is so cool. This is so cool!" How many brain scientists have the opportunity to study their own brain from the inside out?

TIP 66: Pause and stay in character while the audience is laughing.

If you watch great comedians like Bill Cosby, Jerry Seinfeld, or Kathy Griffin, they generally have two modes while they wait in silence for laughter to subside. When they are playing a character, they remain in character with limited or no movement; the exception is when movement is part of the joke. When they get a laugh for something they say when they are not in character, they hold a very mild smile and either stay relatively still or move to a new stage location.

TIP 67: Embed humor in dialogue-rich stories.

Embed humor in your dialogue-rich stories. Rather than describe how she was feeling, Jill Bolte Taylor in the example above expertly incorporated humor in internal dialogue. Similarly, Sir Ken

Robinson placed the humor in the words of Shakespeare's English teacher and Shakespeare's father.

TIP 68: Riff in clusters of three progressively funnier quips.

Learn to riff. If you are wondering how funny you need to be in your TED Talk, consider the extremes. Professional stand-up comics deliver four to five laughs per minute, but that is too many for a keynote, and almost superhuman. In contrast, Bill Gates delivered one laugh every 10 minutes in a TED Talk, and that felt a bit flat.

In my moderately scientific analysis, the most viewed TED speakers deliver an average of just over one laugh per minute. The best ones get around two to three laughs per minute. The secret is that the laughs are not evenly spread out. When they hit a funny theme, the speakers "riff" on the theme with clusters of three, progressively funnier quips. Sir Ken Robinson is the master of this, as illustrated in his young-Shakespeare vignette above.

TIP 69: Amplify humor with vocal, physical, and facial expressiveness.

As speakers, we sometimes forget that we have more than just words at our disposal. With humor there are several nonverbal techniques that can be used to amplify laughs. The simplest adjustments synchronize your facial expressions and your gestures with your humor. Jim Carrey is the greatest contemporary comic genius when it comes to using facial expressions. However, you do not need to get that extreme. Even subtle cues like wide, flashbulb eyes combined with raised eyebrows give your audience the signal to laugh. Since your humor will likely be embedded in stories, show your facial reactions in response to other characters' dialogue. Physicality and movement can have the same amplifying effect. For example, you can make a character appear nervous or skittish through frenetic movement.

TIP 70: Opt for specific rather than generic humor.

Outside of being offensive, there is only one other major aspect of humor to avoid in your public speaking. Avoid telling jokes that you heard or read elsewhere at all costs. This type of joke is often referred to as a public domain joke or a street joke. If your audience has heard this joke before, you will be dismissed as unoriginal. Those who have not heard the joke will instantly sense that it is canned. Telling one-liners is now obsolete, and stand-up comics today concentrate on exaggerating social commentary and personal experiences. This means you should create original humor by dramatizing the characters, events, and dialogue within your personal stories.

Public speaking can be nerve-racking, and trying to get laughs often heightens the anxiety level. But before you fall victim, ask yourself what is the worst that can happen? Perhaps one of your jokes will bomb, and no one will laugh. So what? No one is going to remember. No one is going to talk about your failed attempt at humor at the watercooler. You will not end up destitute. To lower your risk, practice with friends and small audiences before taking the TED stage. This is especially critical, because most humor is discovered during rehearsal rather than written from the start. As with inventions, the secret to getting more laughs is simply to tell a greater number of jokes.

Whether or not a given line gets a laugh depends as much on its content as on how you deliver it. This principle extends, of course, far beyond humor. The next chapter reveals how to master your verbal delivery to enhance your overall message.

CHAPTER 11

Mastering Your Verbal Delivery

TIP 71: Adopt the tone of a passionate one-on-one conversationalist.

To properly grace the TED stage, you must master verbal delivery. Fortunately, you have fertile opportunities to practice, as public speaking is an amplified version of everyday conversation. This, of course, is a double-edged sword because the imperfections that exist in regular speech are magnified during presentations. However, with a small amount of practice, you can transform your verbal delivery both on and off stage.

With the exception of spoken-word artists and classically trained storytellers, most TED speakers tend to adopt the speaking persona of the passionate conversationalist. To pull this off, speak in your own voice with authenticity, interest, and humility. Use clear, everyday, jargon-free language packaged into short, complete sentences. The average TED Talk employs language at a sixth-grade level. Your own enthusiastic interest should shine through with infectious curiosity, wonder, and awe. To demonstrate humility, assume the role

TABLE 11.1

Outline of Steve Jobs's "How to Live Before You Die" Stanford University 2005 Commencement Address

ELEMENT	PREMISE	PROOF
Introduction	(1) "Today, I want to tell you three stories from my life"	
Part A	(3) *Connect the dots.* Follow your heart toward what interests you and trust that it will pay off in the future	(2) I dropped out of Reed College but "dropped in" for 18 months on classes that interested me, such as calligraphy
Part B	(5) *Love and loss:* Don't let failure deter you from what you love	(4) I got fired from the company—Apple—that I started! That led me to NeXT and Pixar
Part C	(7) *Death.* Live each day as if it were your last	(6) A year ago, I was diagnosed with cancer and given three to six months to live, but I was cured with surgery
Conclusion	(8) Stay hungry. Stay foolish	

of a guide who freely shares expertise, not ego. Even the whiff of self-promotion will turn off your audience.

Every so often, TED posts to its website an influential talk given at a third-party forum. Though he never spoke at TED, Steve Jobs exemplified the passionate conversationalist and tops the organization's Best of the Web list. You can witness glimpses of this in his touching Stanford University commencement address in 2005,[1] outlined in Table 11.1, but it is even more evident in his MacWorld addresses in later years. His language is filled with superlatives such as *amazing* and *incredible*. Listening to him, you believed he was trying to challenge the status quo to make the world a better place and you wanted to join his movement.

TIP 72: Eliminate all filler words.

If you have ever tried to eliminate filler words, you know that the process is a lot like trying to fix an old, leaky dam. When you eliminate one, another one pours out of you. Pausing for one beat at commas and two beats at periods will eliminate the most common fillers, including *um, ah, like,* and *you know.*

If you are like most people, your speech is infected with filler words. People use filler words because they are uncomfortable with silence. The most common are *um* and *ah,* but the more evolved have masked these with *so, actually,* and even the occasional lip smack. More insidious, though in the same category, are the words and phrases *like, you know, sort of,* and *kind of* since they express uncertainty—not to mention immaturity—in what you are saying.

The most potent cure for the filler-word plague is the "burst-and-pause" method. Speak in bursts punctuated by pauses. The pause not only replaces filler words but also gives you an aura of self-control. That brief silence provides time to collect and structure your next burst of thoughts. Beyond the personal benefits, the pause gives your audience the time it needs to process what you are saying. Longer pauses add dramatic emphasis like a subtle yet powerful exclamation point and grab an audience's attention. The pause is a gift that keeps on giving.

TIP 73: Exploit the many-faceted power of the pause.

Great speakers like Steve Jobs know that silence is the single most effective vocal technique. In the first minute of his address, Mr. Jobs paused nine times. That works out to one pause every six seconds. And yet his delivery was in no way stilted; quite the opposite in fact. His pauses gave his audience time to savor his message.

Pauses serve four critical purposes and have a fifth special benefit.

The first purpose, to add dramatic effect, is why Mr. Jobs paused for three seconds after taking his place behind the lectern. A portion of the pause allows supporters to finish clapping. However, speakers use the sheer silence to begin developing a deep connection with an audience. They make eye contact with a person or a group of people for a second on the left-hand side. Then they do the same on the right before centering their gaze. Humans are hardwired to increase their attention during silence, and seasoned presenters take every advantage of their audience's evolutionary defense mechanism. The dramatic pause is most often used at the opening of a speech, but it can be used before, during, and more often after, a significant point. That is precisely why Steve Jobs's opening was chockablock with pauses.

The second purpose of the pause is to allow the audience time to process what the speaker is saying. I refer to this as the comprehension pause. Speakers typically pause for one beat—the time it takes to tap your foot once when listening to music—at commas and for two beats at periods. As such, comprehension pauses should be thought of as verbal punctuation marks.

The third purpose for silence was introduced in the chapter on humor. With six instances in his talk, Mr. Jobs demonstrated mastery of the humorous pause. Among those pauses, the most artful was when he remained quiet for eight seconds after saying, "If I had never dropped in on that single course [calligraphy] in college, the Mac would have never had multiple typefaces or proportionally spaced fonts. And since Windows just copied the Mac, it's likely that no personal computer would have them."

The fourth purpose, the transitional pause, is typically longer and allows the speaker to move to a new location on the stage, if desired. At the end of Mr. Jobs's introduction, he paused again to signal the transition into the body of his speech. In this speech, he was not able to move as is his normal custom due to the requirement that he stay behind the lectern.

The fifth, the special benefit, concerns elementary filler words such as *um, ah, like,* and *you know.* When people go on stage, they get nervous. The more nervous they get, the more filler words they utter. Becoming comfortable with silence is the only way to cure the tendency to add filler words. To gain that comfort, practice the comprehension pause by staying quiet at natural breaks in phrases and sentences.

TIP 74: Add vocal variety by varying your speed, volume, and pitch.

Once you have eliminated filler words by mastering the art of the pause, you need to add vocal variety to make your speech interesting. TED Talks require speakers to spend much of their time in the passionate quadrant with delivery that is loud and relatively snappy (see figure). They maintain their volume but slow down to convey major points.

	Slow	**Fast**
Loud	Authoritative	Passionate
Soft	Calming	Suspenseful

VOLUME (vertical axis) · SPEED (horizontal axis)

At transitions, speakers typically move to the calming quadrant. It is a zone subconsciously associated with trust building and is often exploited by salespeople just before they close a deal. Many speakers never venture into the suspenseful quadrant. Those who do use it typically reserve it for portions of stories that have a high degree of anxiety or expectation.

Because human beings are conditioned to detect change, the key to holding audience interest is to use contrast. If your natural manner of speaking is soft and slow, then you can emphasize points by moving to the loud and fast quadrant (passionate), the opposite extreme. The converse is also true; passionate speakers can highlight messages by using a calmer delivery.

There is no optimal quadrant. Any will do as your primary vocal zone. However, you must be careful not to stay in one quadrant too long. If your delivery is unrelentingly passionate, you will overwhelm the members of your audience. They are likely to judge you a zealot and emotionally disconnect. If your delivery is constantly calming, then you will soothe them into boredom. Again, contrast is the key.

The four combinations of volume and speech can be applied to phrases, sentences, and longer passages. However, they can also be applied to individual words. In particular, engaging speakers strive to punch up descriptive adjectives and adverbs with passionate delivery. This is a way to make your energy and enthusiasm infectious.

I like to refer to volume and speed as the primary dimensions of vocal variety since they are the easiest to consciously manipulate. However, I use the words *consciously manipulate* with some trepidation. The reason is because authenticity is the most important characteristic of great public speakers. And authenticity does not take effort. It simply requires you to speak as you would to someone whom you care about.

That is easy to do when you are comfortable. But standing in front of tens, hundreds, or especially thousands of people, causes many presenters to speak in a way that disconnects them from the emotional content of the actual words they are saying. They become somewhat muted and robotic. The best way to reanimate yourself is to amplify the dimensions of your natural delivery until you restore your natural manner of speaking.

After volume and speed, pitch is the next most frequently tuned aspect of vocal variety. With individual words, pitch varies from low to high. In addition, speakers can convey curiosity by gradually increasing pitch to form an upward inflection at the end of a sentence. Note that too many upward inflections come across as sounding juvenile and lacking confidence. Downward inflection, created by lowering the pitch at the end of a sentence, conveys decisiveness and poise.

More subtle dimensions of vocal variety include rhythm, also referred to as cadence or melody, ranging from monotone to dynamic; quality, ranging from breathy to full; and enunciation, ranging from gentle to crisp. In any case, take full, deep breaths and project so that people in the last row can hear you.

Once you master the basics of verbal delivery, going further is mostly counterproductive to effective public speaking. Instead, match the emotional tone (happy, sad, angry, excited, etc.) of a given part of your speech with your delivery. Then crank it up a notch or two—or three for a very large audience—to compensate for the effect of nervousness on your voice. In the next chapter, we turn to the essentials of nonverbal delivery.

CHAPTER 12

Managing Your Nonverbal Delivery

TIP 75: Allow your arms to drop casually when not gesturing.

When I started to develop my public speaking ability, I did not know what to do with my hands. When I consulted reference materials, I either read useless generalizations (do what comes naturally) or lists of what not to do. I yearned for something or someone to tell me what ideal physical delivery looked like.

What I ended up with was this: to be comfortable with what to do with your arms when not gesturing, just do what you do when you are having a conversation while standing up and speaking with somebody you trust. For most people, this means keeping your hands comfortably down at your sides in the moments when you are not using your arms and hands to emphasize a point. This is the most effective base position in public speaking for connecting with your audience as a conversational equal.

Rather than hands down comfortably at their sides with elbows slightly bent, many people believe that the correct base position is to keep their hands above the waist at all times. This stance is appropriate when you wish to appear more authoritative. Others put their hands together at navel level with their fingertips gently touching in the authoritative steeple position; some lace their fingers together; some people keep their hands slightly apart. You can most certainly be an effective speaker if you do any of these, but all are a bit formal unless you are the CEO of a large company or the ruler of your country. Imagine walking around all day, every day, with your hands in any of these positions. It would not be particularly comfortable.

Remember, you would never have a conversation with a person whom you care about with your hands above your waist the entire time, because it creates a barrier. Even at a distance, you will be creating the same barrier with an audience. Whatever rest position you choose, make sure that you are able to maintain symmetry; otherwise your nervous tension becomes obvious to the audience.

Though many rest positions are acceptable, here are several you may find yourself using in normal conversation but you should avoid on stage:

- *Fig leaf.* Holding your arms down but with your hands coupled in front suggests that you are timid.

- *Pockets.* Putting your hands in your pockets makes you appear passive or disinterested.

- *Parade rest.* Holding your arms down but with your hands coupled in back suggests that you are hiding something.

- *Hips.* Placing your hands on your hips makes you appear defiant.

- *Crossed arms.* Crossing your arms is a negative, challenging position.

TIP 76: Assume the model pose when not speaking.

Do you ever feel a bit awkward or uncomfortable when you are on stage but not actively speaking? With years of practice, I am now reasonably comfortable during my presentations. When not moving to a new position, I keep my feet parallel, firmly planted, and shoulder width apart. In the intermittent periods when I am not gesturing, I do one of two things with my arms. In a casual setting, I allow my arms to rest comfortably at my sides. When I need to be more authoritative, I hold my hands in a steeple position at navel level with my fingertips gently touching.

The casual position and the authoritative position are fine and dandy for brief moments, but they both look and feel strange if assumed beyond the 10-second mark. Be aware, because long silences tend to happen naturally at the beginning and at the end of a public speaking performance—when you are being introduced or when you are listening to questions from the audience during Q&A.

I once had the great fortune to receive personal instruction from executive speaking coach Richard Butterfield at a leadership development retreat. When I took the stage in my casual base position described above, Mr. Butterfield sized me up and said, "Do you know that you have assumed an aggressive posture?" Richard explained that the feet-square–arms-down base position in combination with my 6-foot-5, 200-pound frame made me look like a linebacker ready to pounce.

He proceeded to make a subtle adjustment that I immediately recognized as comfortable, casual, and invaluable. I call it the model position—you will understand why once you get into position as follows:

Step 1. Start in the casual position with your feet parallel and shoulder-width apart. Let your arms rest freely at your sides.

Step 2. Bring your right foot forward just a bit so that your feet are still parallel but your left toes are in line with the front of the arch of your right foot.

Step 3. Keeping your right heel in place, pivot the front of your right foot outward at a comfortable angle—about 30 degrees.

Step 4. Rest your weight on your left (back) leg. This will probably cause your front (right) knee to bend a little.

Step 5. Place your left hand in your pocket with your thumb showing. Your right arm will naturally move an inch or two forward. (You may want to test the opposite, with your right hand in your pocket, to see what is more comfortable.)

Don't just read about the steps; stand up and get into position. When you do, you will feel as though you a posing the way a model does. Hence, the "model position." It is relaxed and casual and will simultaneously make you appear confident and approachable.

TIP 77: Gesture naturally and frequently to reinforce your words.

Next, you want to make natural gestures above the waist but below the neck. Unless you are acting out a nervous, self-conscious character in a story, avoid touching your face, head, and hair and the back of your neck. For about half the population, hand gestures are a natural part of the way they converse. If you fit into that group, just keep doing what you are doing. If you are in the other half like me, then you are going to have to force yourself to make hand gestures lest you stand uncomfortably fixed like a tin soldier. It is going to feel awkward initially, but I promise that your discomfort will disappear in no time. The only difference between what you do with your arms in normal conversation versus what you do in public speaking is that you should scale your hand gestures up to suit the size of the room. The bigger your audience, the more dramatic your gestures need to be for people to see them.

Effective hand gestures serve to amplify and support, not overwhelm your story. They should be noticeable neither for their presence nor for their absence. Occasionally you will see speakers repeat the same gesture to the point where it becomes distracting. Though the majority of your gestures should be above the waist and below the neck, you can add variety by occupying the sphere that surrounds you. In context, it is perfectly acceptable to reach to the heavens or to dig into the depths of the earth. When people get nervous, they tend to protect themselves by locking their elbows at their sides. Set your arms free.

When you were a child, your mother likely taught you that pointing is bad manners. Many presenters, however, forget this also applies when speaking to an audience. Pointing is aggressive, if not offensive. What do you do if you desperately need to point? There are two nice alternatives. The first is fist-thumb pointing. Just make a fist with your pinky parallel to the floor and your thumb aimed toward your audience and resting on top of your index finger. This is an effective technique to use, but sparingly, when making an emphatic point. A friendlier, subtler alternative is the palm-up thrust. To execute this, start with your elbow bent and your palm facing upward and then extend your arm toward the audience.

TIP 78: Match your facial expressions to the mood of your content at each moment of your speech.

Effective use of your arms is one component of physical delivery; another is projecting positive body language. For starters, shower your audience with a genuine smile. Smiles communicate calm confidence and build trust between you and your audience. Of course, you cannot smile all the time, so make sure all your facial expressions synchronize with your message.

TIP 79: Maintain three seconds of eye contact with individuals in a random pattern.

Once you master smile and stance, you must develop eye-contact skills. The key to being expert at eye contact is to imagine that you are having a series of conversations with one particular audience member at a time lasting for the duration of one sentence or one thought. Doing this prevents you from continually scanning the audience or staring at the floor or ceiling. This means locking eye contact for three to five seconds with individuals in a random pattern around the room.

You should strive to talk to everybody at least once by the end of your talk. In very large settings, divide the audience into four or more sections and spend as long as one to three minutes speaking to each section as if it were an individual. Make sure that your body is completely facing the individual or section you are speaking to by keeping your head, torso, and legs aligned and your feet planted shoulder-width apart.

Look each person you speak to in one eye, not both. Though I have not seen scientific proof, speaking coaches often recommend looking a person in the left pupil when making an emotional plea and looking the person in the right pupil when making a logical argument. The rationale is that the right side of the brain controls emotions and processes images from the left eye, and the left side of the brain controls logical reasoning and processes images from the right eye, so choose accordingly. If that theory is too out there for you, then just pick an eye and stick with it.

To add variety to eye contact, there is great power in closing your eyes for brief periods. This is appropriate, for example, when you are reminiscing. TED speaker Jill Bolte Taylor uses this technique very effectively at several points in her talk.

Hand gestures, facial expressions, and eye contact are the essential elements of nonverbal communication in one-on-one interactions. When you introduce the stage in public speaking, you have a new consideration to contend with. The next chapter applies the basic elements of theatrical staging to movement during a talk.

CHAPTER 13

Moving Around the Stage

TIP 80: Move within the virtual set you create on stage.

You can transform yourself into a true professional through the use of effective movement. The goal is to make movement fluid and natural while being deliberate. Move with purpose, not simply for variety to free yourself from the tyranny of the lectern and the screen.

To do this, I recommend you visualize the space you will be using as a theatrical stage with defined and consistent locations for the different parts of your speech. If you are telling a story, then each of your characters should occupy a different fixed physical location. If you are explaining a timeline, then start at your audience's left (not your left) and move toward its right as you speak. Note that moving toward your audience is a very powerful technique when emphasizing key points and establishing a deeper personal connection.

Remain in one spot with your body and feet pointing toward your audience as you make a point. Then pause and move during transitions. Begin speaking again once you stop at a new location.

This pause gives your audience time to process your last point and to prepare for your next one. Of course, there are times when you may wish to travel a longer distance. In those instances, speak while moving; however, when you get to your new position, stop and square up your body so that you do not appear to be wandering or pacing.

In his TEDGlobal 2009 talk outlined in Table 13.1, author and former political speechwriter Dan Pink[1] showed what a master he was at movement. The central theme of his talk was to convince businesses to shift their focus from extrinsic rewards to intrinsic incentives to motivate knowledge workers. To support his point, Mr. Pink described an experiment conducted by Princeton University scientist Sam Glucksberg. Here is how Dan Pink set the stage, literally and figuratively:

> He gathered his participants. And he said, "I'm going to time you. How quickly can you solve this problem?" To one group he said, "I'm going to time you to establish norms, averages for how long it typically takes someone to solve this sort of problem."
>
> To the second group he offered rewards. He said, "If you're in the top 25 percent of the fastest times, you get 5 dollars. If you're the fastest of everyone we're testing here today, you get 20 dollars."

When he uttered, "To one group he said . . . ," Mr. Pink moved to his left and gestured to his left. When he said, "To the second group he offered . . . ," he took three giant steps to his right and gestured to the right. Through dialogue, movement, and gestures, Dan Pink brought the experiment to life in the room with sections of the audience as symbolic study participants.

TIP 81: Be deliberate and purposeful in movement.

If you watch TED and especially TEDx Talks delivered by less experienced speakers, you will quickly observe how natural nervousness

TABLE 13.1

Outline of Daniel Pink's "The Puzzle of Motivation" TED Talk

ELEMENT	PREMISE	PROOF
Introduction	(1) I want to make a case for rethinking how we run our businesses	
Part A	(3) Extrinsic rewards like monetary incentives actually reduce productivity for thinking tasks	(2a) Test subjects offered money take longer to solve the abstract problems (2b) Twentieth-century business was built on extrinsic carrot-and-stick motivators
Part B	(5) Knowledge workers are highly motivated by intrinsic rewards	(4) Research from around the world shows that higher incentives lead to lower performance on cognitive tasks
Part C	(6) Future leaders must install a new operating system for motivating workers that centers on autonomy, mastery, and purpose	(7a) Atlassian gives employees "FedEx Days" to work on anything they want for 24 hours (7b) Google gives employees "20% time" (7c) Wikipedia crushed Microsoft Encarta
Conclusion	(8) If we switch from extrinsic to intrinsic motivation, then we can strengthen our businesses and change the world	

on stage gives people a talent for dance they never knew they had. TED curator Chris Anderson is well acquainted with this phenomenon. According to his article "How to Give a Killer Presentation" in the June 2013 *Harvard Business Review*, "The biggest mistake we see in early rehearsals is that people move their bodies too much. They sway from side to side, or shift their weight from one leg to the other."

When working with speakers, I find that most are unaware of what they are doing with their bodies. They are, appropriately, focused on getting their words to come out right. Before giving them any specific advice, I first record them and play back their speech without sound. It takes less than a minute for a speaker to notice precisely how his nervous energy is flowing and to motivate him to address it.

Once people are motivated, the cure is a simple and quick exercise. I ask the speakers to deliver a short speech, usually less than five minutes long, without moving or swaying. I encourage them to redirect their nervous energy into gesturing, vocal intensity, and facial expressiveness. In the most extreme cases, I tap the table with a pen every time the speakers sway their torsos or move their feet. This is irritating and distracting at first but works its magic quickly by affecting the punishment and reward centers in the brain.

TIP 82: Enter and exit the stage with confidence.

There is no shame in being nervous, especially with hundreds of excited audience members anticipating one of the best speeches ever delivered. Public speaking induces anxiety no matter who you are (and anybody who tells you otherwise is flat-out lying). In order to share your idea worth spreading, you must mask your nervousness by channeling your energy into calm confidence. Speakers are judged consciously or subconsciously from the moment they walk onto the stage. For better or worse, everything counts—everything you do from the moment you stand up from your chair to the time you sit down. As you enter and exit the stage, hold your head up, sport a consistently confident smile, and walk with a smooth pace. In most cases, your entrance and exit should not be remarkable either for its timidity or for its exuberance.

The energy level with which you take the stage sends a signal to your audience about the tone of your speech. In TED Talks, the tone is typically inspirational. If you are delivering a somber message, then your pace of movement and your facial expressions should be far more subdued.

At this point, you have all the content and delivery tips you need to deliver an inspiring TED Talk. You may choose to use slides, videos, or props—the focus of the next part of this book—if they are essential to sharing your idea worth spreading.

PART III
DESIGN

CHAPTER 14

Creating Inspiring Slides

TIP 83: Give your talk without slides.

When most people think about TED Talks, they conjure images of elegant, image-rich slide design. While that is certainly true, the best choice you can make in a presentation is to have *no* slides at all. In fact, 4 of the 10 most viewed TED presenters did not use slides, including Sir Ken Robinson,[1] record holder for the highest viewed talk.

One of the main themes of this book is that great speakers drop the pretense, forget all the rules, and use simple and authentic conversational language. You do not prepare slides to speak to friends and family, so try not to use them when you present. As a speaker, you should remove anything that can be construed as a physical or emotional barrier between you and your audience.

TIP 84: Drawing legibly and simply is a great substitute for slides.

If you absolutely, positively need to do something visual, drawing a simple picture is a fantastic alternative to using slides. My personal favorite from the TED universe is Simon Sinek's[2] TEDxPugetSound presentation from 2009. At exactly 2 minutes into his 18-minute talk, Simon walks to a flip chart, picks up a marker, and draws his famous Golden Circle. Imagine a target with three concentric circles. "Why" is in the bull's-eye. "How" is in the middle circle. In the outer circle is "What." This simple drawing illustrates how great leaders inspire and how exceptional companies thrive. You do not need to be a great artist to pull this off. Just make your drawing is simple, obvious, and legible.

TIP 85: When you need to use slides to share data or to document an experience, make them simple, image rich, and text light.

If you absolutely need to share data or to document an experience, then use slides. Keep in mind that the slides are for the benefit of your audience and are not gigantic crib notes for you. Assuming you have the money and the stakes are high, consider using a world-class presentation designer like Nancy Duarte of Duarte Design or Garr Reynolds of Presentation Zen fame. If you cannot afford their services, at least buy and devour their amazing books.

In the best TED Talks that do employ slides, you will find three distinct design approaches known, respectively, as the Godin method, the Takahashi method, and the Lessig method. Though you can be a purist and stick to only one approach in your presentation, I recommend blending two or even three to add contrast and variety. At all costs, avoid using clip art and minimize the use of builds, animation, and video since all these practices take attention away from you.

Entrepreneur and marketing visionary Seth Godin is widely credited with evangelizing the use of image-rich slides. Mr. Godin has spoken at two TED events including TED2003[3] and TED2009.[4] To apply the Godin method, fill an entire slide with a fully licensed photograph of sufficiently high resolution. A nice touch is to have the photograph bleed off the page, thus prompting the people in the audience to use their imagination to complete the picture. Using your own photos that document your story is by far the best option.

If you ignore all my advice and decide to use generic photos, then you should purchase royalty-free images from vendors such as iStockPhoto, Corbis, Getty Images, fotolia, or Shutterstock Images (iStockPhoto, in particular, has a consumer-friendly interface and consumer-friendly pricing).

These photo services offer images in a variety of sizes and file formats that can be daunting to the uninitiated. The rule of thumb is to match the photo size to the resolution of your projector in pixels. If you have an SVGA projector, then 800 × 600 is sufficient. Mainstream projectors today deliver XGA resolution at 1,024 × 768. Better projectors provide SXGA resolution at 1,280 × 1,024.

Sometimes image sizes are represented with inches and dots per inch (dpi). You can treat a dpi as a pixel and simply multiply the inches by the dpi to get the image resolution. For example, a 10-inch × 7.5-inch image at 120 dpi would be 1,200 × 900, which is sufficient for displaying on a 1,024 × 768 XGA projector. Larger images are a waste of money and storage space because you cannot project more pixels than your projector's maximum resolution. As for file format, stick with JPEG, or JPG, which provides the right trade-off in terms of size and quality. PNG is a decent second choice, but avoid GIF (too low quality) and BMP (too bloated).

The second TED-worthy slide design approach available to you is the Takahashi method. Named for Japanese computer programmer Masayoshi Takahashi, this method requires you to build simple slides containing a few words of very large text in a design-enlightened update of the very inelegant 7 × 7 rule. The 7 × 7 rule calls for creating slides with no more than 7 bullets and no more than 7 words per bullet. In comparison to many slides out there, 7 × 7 is a dramatic improvement. However, it is too amateurish for a TED presentation, where bullet points are frowned upon.

The Lessig method is a hybrid of the Godin method and the Takahashi method. This style is named for Stanford University law professor Larry Lessig, who uses a large number of very simple slides in rapid progression. As you have probably guessed, the Lessig method blends a full-screen image with very simple text. For example, if you have a person or an animal looking up and to the right in the image, you place the text in the subject's line of sight.

TIP 86: Emphasize key points using intentional contrast in color, font, or placement.

Regardless of which method you use, the most critical rule of graphic design in slide building is "less is more." Be generous with white space. Strive for each slide to be simple and elegant and for the entire deck to form one harmonious whole. For starters, use the minimum number of words or directly relevant graphics needed to get your point across. Again, your voice is the soundtrack providing additional detail. Minimalism also extends to limiting the number of fonts, colors, and images used. This minimalism also applies to concept density. Great slides have only one "so-what" message. If you have a slide with two-piece charts, split it into two slides. Professional speaking coach Craig Valentine offers a great guideline: "Use slides as a place where you take off and land." Nothing more.

Most designers employ a single font in a design. Since many slides have titles or short key headline-style messages, your best choice is a variant of Helvetica, including its cousin Arial. Every font carries an emotional context, and you should strive to match the typeface to your message. For Helvetica, the mood is neutral yet authoritative— hence a good choice for most presentations. Nearly every sign you see and company logo you come across is constructed with this font.

If you want or need to use multiple fonts, my advice is to stay within the same family. Beyond size, fonts vary in thickness (light, regular, and bold) as well as in other attributes such as italics. All these variations, in addition to the sparing use of a different font color, provide contrast.

The less-is-more rule also applies to the use of color. Choose a limited palette of at most five colors. To maintain consistency among images, fonts, and backgrounds, an excellent practice is to draw the colors from an image or set of images in the presentation. Many of the most effective palettes are actually monochromatic, where the color (hue) stays the same but the lightness and darkness (tone or value) and brightness and dullness (saturation) vary. Alternatively, you can go for subtle but clear contrast with an analogous color scheme, one in which colors are adjacent on a color wheel. For bold contrast, to be used sparingly, employ complementary colors that sit on opposite sides of the color wheel. Neutral colors like black and white may also be suitable for backgrounds. When presenting data, use a solid color that does not interfere with the message.

In addition to the less-is-more philosophy, another set of principles worth internalizing is the attentive placement of text and images. Again, this is the stuff of design community battles, but I recommend that you apply the rule of thirds. Just divide a slide into a three-by-three grid of nine equal-size boxes, using this grid to align both text and images. It is perfectly acceptable, and accepted, for elements to span multiple boxes, but do so with awareness and intention. For example, imagine that you consumed an entire slide with a single nature photograph. In that case, you would align the horizon with one of the two horizontal grid lines. If the sky is dull, align it with the top one. If dramatic, then align the horizon with the bottom grid line.

The grid is your guide to the focal points on the slide. There are five of them. The first four are at the intersections of the grid lines and make excellent places to place an image. The fifth is more subtle and is at the visual center of the slide just up and to the right of true center.

Just before I sat down to write this chapter, my 12-year-old daughter was working on a presentation about the volcanic island Krakatoa using Prezi, a storyboarding tool with professional graphics including panning and zooming. In the other room, my 9-year-old son was using PowerPoint to write his book report on Lois Lowry's *Number the Stars.* As proud as I am of the fact that my children are learning design skills at an early age, I could not help but shed a small tear that they had developed a disproportionate amount of pride in their slide transitions and animations as compared with their content. I suspect that my children are not alone in this regard and that I am not the only parent trying to reverse the technology-enabled triumph of style over substance.

I hope that you take my advice to heart and develop the ability to speak without using slides. This is a skill that is becoming increasingly valuable as it becomes increasingly scarce. At present, I can only think of two acceptable exceptions to not using slides.

One exception is when you have personal photos that greatly enrich your talk. Pictures in this category document your experience, and each is truly worth a thousand words. Note that this exception has two parts. The first is that you use personal photos rather than stock photos, or worse, clip art. The second is that the photos actually enrich your talk. Slides, even ones with images, force listeners to turn off their imagination. That is a hefty price to pay and should be worth the trade-off.

The other exception is when you present data. Again, the data should be your data, and they should enrich your talk in a way that words cannot. Especially with data, apply the techniques in this chapter to keep your slides simple and focused.

Some speakers need to go a step further than slides and use video clips. With the same caveats that the videos be your videos and that they must add value to your talk, we turn to multimedia in the next chapter.

Using Video Effectively

TIP 87: Keep your video clips short.

Since TED frowns heavily on commercial promotion, the organization rarely selects speakers from traditional corporate backgrounds who talk to promote what they do. Moreover, given the conventional wisdom that all advertising is evil, one would not expect to see the vice chairman of one of the world's largest marketing agencies on the main stage. Rory Sutherland[1] of Ogilvy & Mather UK broke through by promoting ways to use advertising for good. The outline of his talk is provided in Table 15.1.

In addition to his 22 slides, Rory also used two videos. The first was a 30-second commercial ending with this voice-over: "New Diamond Shreddies cereal. Same 100 percent whole-grain cereal in a delicious diamond shape." The video was short and sweet and led to a big laugh as the audience absorbed the irony that diamonds are just squares rotated by 45 degrees.

After a few remarks, he showed a 65-second video of focus group participants responding to the new cereal in a market research

TABLE 15.1

Outline of Rory Sutherland's "Life Lessons from an Ad Man" TED Talk

ELEMENT	PREMISE	PROOF
Introduction	(1) Intangible value is a fine substitute for using up labor or limited resources	(2) Instead of spending £6 billion to shave 40 minutes off a rail commute, what if we simply entertained people
Part A	(3) Most problems are problems of perception	(4) Placebo medicine, placebo education, royal potatoes, compulsory veil wearing, and orange juice
Part B	(5) Persuasion is better than compulsion	(6) Radar speed signs are a less resource-intensive and equally effective way to get people to slow down as compared with handing out speeding tickets
Part C	(7) Embracing intangible value allows us to conserve our limited resources	(8) Prussian jewelry, Shaker minimalism, denim clothing, and Coca-Cola
Part D	(9) The new media ecosystem allows massively decentralized value creation that can be used for good	(10) Food and drink examples and big red savings button in your home
Part E	(11) Appreciate the value in tangible goods that already exist	(12) Shreddies cereal and low-priced wine
Conclusion	(13) Appreciate the value of intangibles like health and love	

study. Though at times hilarious, this video felt a little long. Either through nature or nurture, humans are accustomed to watching video interruptions in 30-second segments. Rory could have either dropped this second video or cut it by 50 percent.

Comedian Charlie Todd,[2] whom you met in Chapter 2 on organizing your talk, was an expert at utilizing videos. Using one video in a presentation can be distracting for an audience, but showing four can be 10 times more distracting, so it should be done with extreme caution. Mr. Todd handled this expertly by showing videos with generally decreasing duration starting with his longest at 180 seconds, followed by one at 65 seconds, then 77 seconds, and finally 50 seconds. Using progressively shorter videos provides the audience with a satisfying feeling that the talk is accelerating.

TIP 88: Stand to the side and watch videos that have high-quality audio.

Rory Sutherland's two videos were a complete audiovisual experience that fully absorbed his audience's attention. If he had tried to narrate, then listeners would have neither comprehended him nor his multimedia content. Rather than look out into the audience or stare at his confidence monitor (a display facing the presenter), Rory Sutherland wisely stood silently off to one side and turned to watch the same large screen as his audience.

TIP 89: Narrate videos that lack audio.

In contrast to Rory's approach, Charlie Todd narrated his videos. This is the right approach when the audio track consists of low-level background noise. Moreover, narration is critical for videos that run longer than one minute, as was the case with three of Mr. Todd's four videos. In addition to performing artists like Charlie, inventors frequently show and narrate videos to demonstrate the technologies they have created.

You will never see a TED video with a multimedia glitch, since problems are edited in postproduction. However, I can pretty much guarantee that you will see a minor or major issue with video at most TEDx events. The problem is that video has a habit of working perfectly fine on your computer but will misbehave for various reasons when shown using a projector and sound system. For this reason I advise speakers in smaller venues to avoid video altogether. In the event that the video is critical to your talk, then arrive at the venue early and play your videos in full prior to the event.

You have probably detected my bias against slides and videos unless they add significant value and document your personal experience. Props are another design element that represents a good complement or alternative, and the next chapter shows you how to use them effectively.

CHAPTER 16

Using Props

TIP 90: Hide your props when not in use.

Though a rarity outside of technical demonstrations, using contextually relevant props is a great way to mix things up during a presentation. During his TED Talk outlined in Table 16.1, antipoverty activist Bunker Roy[1] donned a hand puppet to share how he uses it to solve disputes in the villages he advises:

> *Where the percentage of illiteracy is very high, we use puppetry. Puppets is the way we communicate. You have Jokhim Chacha who is 300 years old. He is my psychoanalyst. He is my teacher. He's my doctor. He's my lawyer. He's my donor. He actually raises money, solves my disputes. He solves my problems in the village. If there's tension in the village, if attendance at the schools goes down and there's a friction between the teacher and the parent, the puppet calls the teacher and the parent in front of the whole village and says, "Shake hands. The attendance must not drop." These puppets are made out of recycled World Bank reports.*

Mr. Roy kept this hand puppet on a nearby lectern. Following best practice, it would have been somewhat more effective had he

TABLE 16.1

Outline of Bunker Roy's "Learning from a Barefoot Movement" TED Talk

ELEMENT	PREMISE	PROOF
Introduction	(2) There is more to life than comfort	(1) *Ordinary world.* After graduating from the best schools 45 years ago, I was set up for a comfortable future. But I got curious what it was like to live and work in villages
Part A	(4) The knowledge of traditional village professionals has incredible value beyond the confines of their communities	(3) *Inciting incident.* So I dug wells in rural India for five years and dreamed of starting a "Barefoot College" to empower the poor to share traditional knowledge and skills
Part B	(6) If you empower villagers with even more knowledge, then they can improve lives in their communities	(5) *Climax.* Until one day in 1986, we ultimately built the Barefoot College to provide education, food, shelter, electricity, and medical care
Part C	(8) The best practices of rural villagers are transferable within and between countries	(7) *New normal.* And our approach was so effective, that we spread the methods to women across India, Africa, and Afghanistan
Conclusion	(9) Therefore, the people on the ground have all the solutions they need at their fingertips	

hidden the prop before and after using it. Many TED speakers have an assistant deliver and remove a prop. Alternatively, he could have put the puppet in a small, nondescript box to keep the audience from being mildly distracted by it.

It is also notable that Mr. Roy not only used the hand puppet but also had slides of the puppet being used in village settings. I found this to be a novel, clever, and effective combination.

TIP 91 : Use props sparingly.

Unless absolutely necessary, strive to use a single prop, since using many props can get gimmicky. Bunker Roy used only his puppet, Jokhim Chacha. Similarly, Jill Bolte Taylor held up a real human brain complete with dangling spinal cord as she explained the biological function of the right and left hemispheres.

TIP 92 : Ensure your props are large enough to be visible to your audience.

Because props are most frequently used in technical demonstrations, large, well-produced venues like TED and TEDGlobal often use a video camera or two to zoom in on the prop and project it on ultralarge screens. So prop size really is not an issue. However, in smaller venues such as TEDx events, props should be large enough for every audience member to get a good look. If a prop is too small, then you can resort to showing a video of your prop in action, as Pranav Mistry[2] did when showcasing his various computer-human interface devices.

One way to make your prop visible to your audience is to make it fly, as Markus Fischer[3] did in his TEDGlobal 2011 talk entitled "A Robot That Flies Like a Bird." After explaining briefly that he worked with a team to build an ultralight SmartBird modeled after the herring gull, an assistant launched a large robotic bird with a two-meter wingspan from the back of the room. As the bird flew above the audience for 40 seconds, Mr. Fischer remained silent and tracked it with the same expression of wonder that his audience exhibited. Once the flight ended and he began speaking again, he held a full-scale replica of the SmartBird that had its skin removed so that the audience could see the robot's mechanical innards.

When most people think about design in the context of public speaking, they think only about slides, videos, and props. However, there is another rarer design element that occupies the stage—the lectern. As you will discover in the next chapter, lecterns can be used intentionally to establish authority or as a crutch for less-confident speakers.

CHAPTER 17

Using a Lectern

TIP 93: Use a lectern when you need to project authority.

Though rare on the TED stage, lecterns are neither purely good nor purely evil. Several outstanding speakers, including Chimamanda Adichie[1] and Karen Thompson Walker[2] used them. (As every commentator on this topic has done before me, I offer the gentle reminder that a podium is a stage you stand on and a lectern is a stand you speak behind.)

Let's start by assuming that you have practiced your material and have your content and delivery solidly nailed. In that case, you are simply making a stylistic decision about whether or not to use a lectern. In most cases, the best choice is to avoid using one entirely because it creates a physical and psychological barrier between you and your audience. If your goal is to motivate and inspire, the lectern is your enemy.

The first reason to use a lectern is when you intentionally need to project power and authority. In years past, executives always spoke from behind lecterns. Today, they reserve the lectern for more solemn occasions such as sharing financial performance or delivering bad news. When your objective is authority, remember to maintain consistency in your other actions. When not using a lectern, President Barack Obama frequently leaves his jacket behind and rolls up his sleeves. However, when he speaks from behind a lectern, he always wears a formal suit and tie with the jacket buttoned.

To maintain authority, make sure that you and the lectern are completely out of the line of fire of projected slides or images. It is also hard to command authority if you are very short relative to the height of the lectern, so either use a discrete step stool or avoid using the lectern.

A second reason to use a lectern is dictated by the norms of the event or the audience. For example, some churches require that speakers talk from behind a lectern to project teaching authority. In this circumstance, the lectern also makes it easier to read long passages from a religious text. The same logic holds true when delivering a eulogy.

A third reason to use a lectern is when you need to rely on notes and you do not have a teleprompter available. In most instances, this is a poor justification—with sufficient practice you should not need notes. However, if you speak often and on a wide range of topics, you simply may not have the time to rehearse adequately. In addition, there are situations when the stakes are very high and every word matters, as is the case when a CEO is issuing an apology for a consumer product safety recall.

TIP 94: Rest your hands gently on the lectern.

From what I see, the majority of untrained speakers grip the sides of the lectern. Even more egregious are those speakers who grab its front or back edges or rest their elbows on any part of it.

If those are the worst practices, what are the best practices? Every time you speak, you should determine ahead of time your default or base hand position. This means knowing exactly where you are going to place your hands when you are not gesturing. I recommend comfortably resting your hands on the lectern, especially if you are referring to notes. Any of the following three ways are acceptable. The most casual approach is with your hands fully interlaced with the webbing of the fingers of your right hand touching the webbing of the fingers of your left hand. When doing so, be careful not to clench too tightly. The intermediate approach is to interlace your hands so that the fingertips of each hand touch the webbing of the other hand with palms apart. Most speakers who apply this technique allow their thumb tips to touch. The formal approach is to pair the fingertips of both hands, pinky with pinky, pointer with pointer, and so on.

If you are not referring to notes, then another acceptable base position is to stand about a foot behind the lectern and use a steeple position with your hands in front of you at navel level.

Regardless of whether you choose to rest your hands on the lectern or hold them at navel level, gesture normally and confidently at or above chest level. By way of reference, this is a bit higher than when speaking without a lectern due to the obvious obstruction. Also, unless you are a crazed dictator, please do not pound the lectern. If you are a crazed dictator, then pound early and often.

TIP 95: Move away from the lectern if you can.

To break the physical and psychological barrier between you and your audience, move away from the lectern if you can. Your ability to do so will be limited by the formality of the occasion, by audio-video considerations, and by your degree of preparation.

In very formal settings, start, deliver, and end your speech without venturing out from behind the lectern. That means that you need to keep your feet planted firmly, square, and straight for what is likely to be a long time. Of course, you can shift your weight occasionally, and I do mean occasionally, for comfort. Also remember not to lean toward or on the lectern or to rock your body.

Audio and video considerations may also inhibit your ability to move around. Most obviously, if the only available microphone is attached to the lectern, then you are stuck. Additionally, if your talk is being broadcast over a simple, single camera video feed, then your range of movement is limited, if not nonexistent, due to the mechanics of tracking and focus.

If the occasion is not overly formal and you have a wireless microphone with either no video or a very sophisticated video setup, then you are free to move about the cabin. Though you may choose to start and end your speech from behind the lectern, move with purpose and with pseudotheatrical staging in mind. That means that you are not solely moving for variety or comfort, nor are you moving to release your nervous energy.

If you move, really move. Do not remain artificially tethered to the lectern by stepping just to its right, left, or front. Another amateurish maneuver is to return to the lectern simply to advance your slides or refer to your notes. Use a wireless slide changer; preferably a very simple one that you can surreptitiously advance by pressing on your pocket. If you do lose your place and need to come back to look at your notes, then do so while taking a drink of water. This clever sleight of hand distracts your audience from your true purpose, but doing this excessively will both undermine your credibility and hasten your need for a bathroom break.

When you do leave the lectern, do so without taking your notes, water, or any other materials so you leave the stage with confidence and authority. You can always come back for them at intermission or get them from your host.

TIP 96: Use notes like a professional.

As I mentioned before, the best use of notes is to use no notes at all. That said, my observation is that 99 percent of speakers who use a lectern use notes. If you insist on being in this majority, you might as well use notes correctly.

Your best option is to use a single-page outline printed in very large font on the upper half of the page only. Avoid using ALL CAPS since that is much more difficult to read. In addition, leave the clear sheet protector at home (or hide it before you start) since it tends to reflect light and produce glare.

If you do need multiple pages of notes, apply the same best practices that you would for a single page. In addition, keep the pages loose (not stapled together or in a three-ring binder) and clearly number them in case you drop them. Finally, advance the pages by sliding them over rather than flipping them to minimize movement and noise so you do not distract your audience from your message.

If you need to speak and project authority behind a lectern, then I strongly encourage you to practice at a lectern and come as close as possible to simulating your ultimate situation. At a minimum, plan in advance your default hand position and any other potential movement. If you are prepared, your muscle memory will naturally take over and leave you free to focus on your message and your audience.

CHAPTER 18

Dressing for Success on Stage

TIP 97: Select an appropriate outfit in advance of the event.

The clothing you wear during your talk can affect your performance and its reception by your audience. Consequently, do not leave selecting, cleaning, or buying your outfit to the evening before or the day of your performance. Instead, assemble your outfit a few days in advance so that you can focus your attention on polishing your content and delivery.

The single most important consideration for dressing for success on stage is that the clothes you wear make you feel physically comfortable. Most people are more at ease wearing clothes that are slightly loose fitting. Because stage lighting can be hot, choose breathable natural fabrics like cotton or light wool. If your feet are not happy, your discomfort can show, so select a pair of shoes that are broken in but polished. The clothes and shoes you are in should be something you are comfortable wearing all day. Physical comfort and confidence go hand in hand.

Women have more clothing options than men, so ladies need to factor in some additional considerations. The first few rows of your audience will usually be below you, and there may be balcony seating above you. Depending on the production, you may have cameras focused on you from many angles. Additionally, stage lighting will render sheer clothing more transparent; what works in the dim lighting of your home or office may become a wardrobe malfunction on stage. For these reasons, I advise women to wear outfits with appropriate coverage and length. And ladies, unless you are a seasoned expert at walking in high heels, opt for low heels or flats.

Your outfit should match your personality and the tone of your talk: Consider the clothing choices of several TED speakers. In a traditional burgundy kurta (a long-sleeved tunic extending to just below the knees), brown-wool vest, and loose-fitting white pants, Bunker Roy[1] looked the part of a man advocating for the empowerment of the poor in India. Amanda Palmer,[2] an edgy musician, exuded her persona in a gray T-shirt with a subtle floral silk-screened pattern, dark-gray jeans with the hems turned up, black combat boots, and chunky accessories. Matching his material and his professorial aura, education advocate Sir Ken Robinson[3] wore a suit coat and slacks with a light-gray shirt but no tie. All these speakers chose clothing that expressed who they were in a nondistracting way.

Within the confines of your persona, strive to dress one degree more formally than your audience. At a more casual event like a TEDx, you should dress in business casual at the very least. At a TED event where the audience will mostly be wearing business casual, opt for business professional. Men generally cannot go wrong with a dark suit and solid-white shirt, tie optional. Dark suits also work well for women, as do dresses with jackets. As for color choice, it is a good idea to check with the organizer to find out what color backdrop is being used so that you do not match it exactly and blend in. Finally, avoid stripes and loud patterns since they are distracting to the audience and do not show up well on camera.

TIP 98: Ensure your outfit is microphone-ready.

If you are speaking in a venue with more than 20 people, the odds are good that you will be wearing a wireless lavalier microphone. In some instances, you will actually need to wear two of these, one for the speakers and one for the camera. These clip-on microphones are attached to a chunky transmitter with a cable. You should be mindful of the impact this may have when deciding on your outfit. A few things to consider:

First, you will need to clip the transmitter somewhere. Before you dismiss this as trivial, I have had many harrowing moments as a TEDx organizer trying to figure out where to place the transmitter. In one case, a speaker was wearing a skin-tight dress, flimsy decorative belt, and no jacket. My brilliant cameraman Desmond Horsfield improvised by taping the transmitter to the back of the woman's dress just before she took the stage. Men and women can avoid this by wearing a jacket, pants, or a sturdy belt.

Second, you will need somewhere to clip on the microphone. The ideal placement is as close to the center of your body as possible and six to eight inches below your chin. This is yet another reason why I encourage male and female speakers to wear a jacket. If a jacket does not work for you, make sure that whatever shirt, blouse, or dress you are wearing has a sturdy and convenient place to clip on the microphone. These microphones are very sensitive, so make sure to place them where your hair, jewelry, or fabric will not brush up against them. If you are lucky, your event organizer may provide you with an ear-worn microphone. This attaches over the ear and extends across your face, allowing far more flexibility in your choice of clothing and jewelry.

Third, you will need to hide the cable that links the transmitter to the clip-on microphone. Once again, a jacket is your best option, with the cable running up your back and over your shoulder. If you aren't wearing a jacket, prepare yourself, because someone you do not know very well is going to help you snake the cable through your clothing.

If possible, it is a good idea to do a sound check before the event starts or during a break. This will allow you to make minor adjustments and build your confidence. Make sure your pockets are empty during the sound check and during your performance, and avoid walking directly in front of an audio speaker.

TIP 99: Bring a backup outfit.

In high-stakes speaking situations, especially those involving cameras, bring a backup outfit that you can change into quickly in the event of a wardrobe malfunction or a spill. It is also good to have a sewing kit on hand in case you lose a button.

It is very easy to throw yourself into a tailspin while preparing for a presentation. The aspect to pay the most attention to is your content. Make your clothing selection a nonissue by dressing as your authentic self in comfortable attire suited to your profession.

PART IV

THE JOURNEY TO THE STAGE AND BEYOND

CHAPTER 19

Getting Selected to Give a TED Talk

TIP 100: Live your passion.

"How do I get picked to give a TED Talk?" is the most frequently asked question I hear, especially from professional speakers. I have to admit though that this is a chapter I did not want to write because I think it is based on a dangerous premise. When you ask this question, you lose sight of what really matters—living your life in the authentic embrace of an idea worth spreading. If you give a TED Talk but do not live your passion, then you have lost the game. If you live your passion and never give a TED Talk, then you win. And not surprisingly, living your passion is the most direct path to giving a TED Talk.

Throughout this book, I have endeavored to give you concrete how-to tips on delivering a memorable TED Talk, but on this particular subject, I refer you to others far more qualified than I, such as Seth Godin for achieving your professional passion, Oprah Winfrey for living your personal passion, or Tony Robbins who blends the two. I also want you to think about the three groups—educators, entertainers, and change agents—of 15 personas that I highlighted in Chapter 1. With few exceptions, these people have devoted decades of their lives to the study and mastery of a single, often esoteric, field. That they gave a TED Talk along their journey is just a period at the end of a sentence, and that sentence is just one tiny part of the story of their lives.

Perhaps my own story will be illuminating. By way of backstory, I had been studying and practicing public speaking for more than 10 years. Along the way, I kept getting advice saying that I should strive to be an expert who speaks rather than an expert speaker. The former has great depth of content; the latter just has a silver tongue. However, as much as I explored various domains, I kept coming back to my total fixation on speaking. To the best of my knowledge, speaking about speaking generally does not pay the bills, but, fortunately, I had a day job.

In December 2011, my friend Sarah Goshman asked a group of fellow Toastmasters to help her organize a TEDx event. At the time, Sarah was working as a jack-of-all-trades at Jacob's Cure, a tiny not-for-profit dedicated to curing Canavan disease. (Canavan disease is a genetic neurological disorder that incapacitates children and then takes them in the first decade of life.) Outside her day job, Sarah is an experience seeker. She knew that TEDx organizers are strictly prohibited from self-promotion, but she got caught up in the TED phenomenon and wanted to do something to help spread ideas in her local community.

Though I did not know anything about organizing events, I volunteered to help her fill out the roster of speakers from my immediate and extended network. As the event approached, Sarah needed to step back into a supporting role to free up time to care for an ailing relative. Being her second in command, I stepped up to fill the gap as lead organizer and emcee.

In the audience on the day of the event was a group of "twentysomethings" who worked together in Hartford, Connecticut, including insurance business analyst Brian Waddell. At the end of the day, Brian and friends decided they wanted to put on their own TEDx event and asked me if I wanted to speak about speaking. I guess my attempt to be a minimal presence and simply introduce speakers and connect their talks to our theme did not mask my speaking nerd bat signal. If you ever meet me, you will see for yourself that I have a hard time turning it off.

The point of my story is not that organizing a TEDx event is a good way to speak at TEDx or TED. In fact, it is a terrible way because organizers are prohibited by TED from speaking at their own events. Moreover, planning and executing an event is a time-consuming, stressful, and costly endeavor. My point is that I had absolutely no intent to speak at a TEDx event. I was living my passion, a random set of dominoes fell, a TEDx organizer invited me to speak, and I said yes. Substitute the particular obsession, and you will find that nearly every TED or TEDx speaker has a similar story.

TIP 101: Get friendly with an in-demand speaker.

When it came time to find speakers for the first TEDx event that I helped organize, I aimed high and sent the following e-mail to marketing visionary Seth Godin:

> *Hi Seth: I am organizing a TEDx event in Stamford, CT on April 28th. Though I appreciate that the audience may be a bit small for you (~100), are there any speakers in the NYC metro area that you are mentoring and would like to pass this opportunity to? Regards, Jeremey*

I sent that e-mail at 9:54 p.m. on a Tuesday night. Bear in mind that Seth and I do not know each other, and yet he replied three minutes later to connect me with meeting culture warrior Al Pittampalli. Al recommended another speaker who recommended another speaker. Even after we had locked down our agenda, Seth referred two more speakers—Lauryn Ballesteros and Ishita Gupta— whom I then referred to another TEDx organizer. Al, Lauryn, and Ishita were not seeking a speaking opportunity; they were living their passions in a way that caught the eye of someone who gets too many invitations and is remarkably devoted to helping others succeed.

TIP 102: When all else fails, apply to speak.

For both TED and TEDx events, you are much more likely to be invited to speak by an organizer who notices you than you are to get selected through an open application process. That said, it cannot hurt to apply since the worst the organizer can do is say no.

As you would imagine, it is much harder to speak at TED or TEDGlobal than it is to speak at an independently organized TEDx event. The official TED Conference has held open auditions in the past, but the process changes from year to year. TED has a "Suggest a Speaker" form where people can nominate themselves or be nominated by others. Just to set your expectations, I have never met a speaker whose journey to the stage started by filling out this form. Though it is the wrong reason to go to TED, there are several speakers, including, but not limited to, Becky Blanton,[1] Richard St. John,[2] and Cindy Gallop,[3] who were initially attendees and who were later invited to give talks.

There are over 1,000 TED Talks online and more than 25,000 TEDx Talks. By that measure, your odds are 25 times better of getting an opportunity to speak at TEDx. Here is what John Jeffrey Mardlin, cofounder of TEDxVictoria, said on Quora.com about the informal TEDx application process:

> For TEDx events, in my experience as an organizer, we don't mind people pitching their talk ideas to us. However, most people don't seem to have a very good conception of how to give a short

"TED style" talk. A large number of people that approach TED
and TEDx organizers turn out to be self-promoters. The best talks
are usually given by people who are too busy doing their awesome
work to propose a talk. We have to go get them and convince them
to dedicate a considerable amount of time to spreading their ideas.

Some suggestions if you plan to audition: Be focused. Tell us
about something only you can tell us about. Don't pitch your proj-
ect, teach us what you know because of it.

Please don't tell us about a general trend in the world, such as
the dawning of a new age of consciousness where humans learn
to move beyond capitalism, consumerism and begin to love one
another and the planet. That may be true, but what makes you
qualified to tell us that? It's about Ideas, but there needs to be
experience, research or at least narrative behind it.

My experience mirrors Mr. Mardlin's. What he describes as
"self-promoters" are often professional speakers and trainers. Some
of my closest friends speak for a living and dream of speaking at
TED or TEDx. Though I have deep respect for them, I warn them
that the content that sells to people who pay for corporate speaking engagements does not have the novelty and raw authenticity
needed for a TED Talk. My best advice to them is that they should
not change who they are; after all, they are pursuing their passion!
However, when they apply to speak, I recommend that they focus on
sharing a story with an idea worth spreading from their "normal,"
nonspeaking life.

Perhaps the worst possible reason to speak at TED is to use it as a
springboard to catapult to fame and fortune. Though you can find
examples of people whose careers blossomed after delivering a TED
Talk, the likelihood of this happening and the degree of control are
akin to winning the lottery. My life did not change after my TEDx
Talk, or at least not due to my speech. Wait, you say, didn't it lead
to this book? Funnily enough, no! I self-published an early version

of this book long before I gave my TEDx Talk. Moreover, my TEDx Talk has an insignificant number of views, which just goes to show that speaking about speaking is not the world's most popular topic.

Similarly, I have spoken to people whose talks have hundreds of thousands and even millions of views. Some of these people were famous to begin with, and the TED experience was just another log on the fire. For others, their phones rang and their inboxes filled up for a couple of weeks, maybe a month or two; then life went back to normal, and they continued to pursue their passion.

Again, the right reason to give a TED Talk is to share an idea worth spreading. If an organizer chooses you (or if you get the opportunity to give a speech in another venue), then you are going to need to prepare. The next chapter will help you do that.

CHAPTER 20

Preparing Without Fear

TIP 103: Practice your talk a minimum of three times in a feedback-rich environment.

Controlling public speaking anxiety actually begins long before the day of your presentation. In particular, if you are giving a TED Talk, you should practice a minimum of three times in a safe, feedback-rich environment. A single expert speaker qualifies as providing a feedback-rich environment, though you may wish to gather a small group of your friends and peers. Your goal is to speak conversationally and avoid memorizing or reading from a script. Practicing three times will give you the needed familiarity and confidence with your content to do that.

Presenting in front of a group of friends or going to a Toastmasters meeting trumps the commonplace advice of speaking to the mirror, reading your speech to yourself, or listening to your speech over and over. Because it simulates a real setting, you are more likely to actually practice once you commit to a scheduled practice time.

Also, there is something about the pressure of speaking in front of other people that sears a speech into your brain.

Unless you have stage acting experience, I recommend that you outline your talk rather than scripting it out verbatim. Even if you are able to memorize a large amount of material, memorized speeches always sound inauthentic. Moreover, if you lose your place, it is much harder to recover than if you are working from an outline. Each time you practice your speech, it will be a little bit different and a little bit better.

TIP 104: Arrive early at the venue to gain comfort with the logistics and with the audience.

Your fear will likely intensify when you arrive at the venue. Public speaking is a performance given before an audience. Just as stage directors ensure that everything is ready before the curtain goes up on a play, great presenters take control of their environment. Arrive early to have adequate time to assimilate or modify the technology and physical space.

If you are using technology, leave no stone unturned. Always have a "plan B," such as a one-page outline (preferred) or a printed copy of your slide deck. Test your microphone. Run through your slides in presentation mode to ensure the computer is functioning and that graphics are displaying as expected. It is easy to fall into complacency. Once, I inserted a graphic of an innocent-enough stop sign into a presentation and did not perform a dry run. To my shock and horror, the stop sign began flashing obnoxiously in a presentation before the senior leaders of my company. Fortunately, they had a sense of humor, but I learned that you can never be too careful.

Understanding and even changing your environment is just as important as testing the technology. Regardless of whether or not you can alter your environment, you should always take the time to plan how you will use the physical space. For example, if you have the freedom to move around while speaking, you can determine where to stand and which pathways to take. If you can alter the environment, you might choose to reconfigure chairs and tables, add or remove a podium, or reposition a movable whiteboard.

Arriving early to gain control of the environment gives you confidence that will carry over into your presentation. However, there is yet another compelling benefit. Once you have mastered the technology and the physical space, arriving early gives you a golden opportunity to build rapport with your audience before you speak formally. By listening carefully, you will create allies and be able to draw their insights and stories into your speech.

TIP 105: Remember that your audience wants you to succeed.

To release nervous energy just before you take the stage, shake your hands and arms vigorously—assuming you are out of sight of your audience. Next, take slow, deliberate diaphragmatic breaths that expand your stomach when you breathe in and contract your stomach when you breathe out; if you are doing this right, your shoulders will not move. Additionally, keep your notes in your pocket. You will probably never need them, but having them there will settle your subconscious fears. And follow the practice of professional speakers by emptying your pockets of everything other than your notes before taking the stage.

As you start your actual presentation, remember that the audience truly wants you to succeed. Though I do not recommend memorizing your entire presentation, I do advise memorizing your introduction. When you start strong, your confidence carries forward.

Finally, remember that nervous speakers have a tendency to speak too fast. Slow down and make liberal use of pauses. Pauses give your audience time to catch up with your message and also give you the time to take slow, deliberate breaths. (Pauses are also part of the "burst-and-pause" method cure for the filler-word plague discussed in Chapter 11.)

TIP 106: Request a confidence monitor.

Confidence monitors, the displays that face the presenter, are essential for anyone giving a high-stakes presentation. If you have slides, then the confidence monitor allows you to continue looking forward as you advance your slides. This will both lower your blood pressure and make you appear more polished since you will not need to constantly turn to check the screen.

Confidence monitors are equally valuable when giving a talk without slides. The event organizer should be able to put whatever you want on the monitor. I recommend an ultrasimplified, large-text outline that fits on a single page, since it would be strange for you to have a wireless slide changer when your audience cannot see any slides. Odds are that you will not need it, but it is reassuring to have in case you do. Even if there is someone to advance the slides, you do not want to rely on anyone to synchronize you with your presentation.

Fear of public speaking is real and universal, and classifying it as rational or irrational does not make it go away. Knowing that other speakers also view public speaking as a fate worse than death does not help make it any less frightening. As I said earlier, speaking anxiety never goes away; you simply learn to channel the energy into passionate delivery through regular practice.

CHAPTER 21

Being Introduced Effectively

TIP 107: Write a one- to two-minute introduction for your emcee that connects to your core message.

Unfortunately, TED videos do not show the manner in which speakers are introduced. There is also not much in the way of information on the "TED way" for speaker introductions in the public domain. Though a bad introduction will probably not sink a great talk, a great introduction of no longer than a minute or two has the ability to provide a powerful launch into your speech.

One of the most viewed TED speakers is Hans Rosling, who manages to vibrantly bring life to otherwise dull reams of public health data. His core message is that we can join together to raise global health standards by freely sharing public health data and analytical tools. Let me start out by showing you what an ineffectual introduction to Hans's revolutionary talk might have sounded like:

Ladies and gentlemen. Today, it is my pleasure to introduce
Dr. Hans Rosling, professor of international health at Karolinska

Institute in Stockholm. In his early academic career, Dr. Rosling studied statistics and medicine, ultimately becoming a licensed physician in 1976. As a result of his discovery and subsequent investigation of an outbreak of konzo, a paralytic disease, Hans earned his PhD from Uppsala University in 1986. He has won over 10 prestigious awards, including the Gannon Award in 2010 for the continued pursuit of human advancement. In 2011 Dr. Rosling was ranked one of the 100 most creative people in business by Fast Company *magazine and was elected as a member of the Swedish Academy of Engineering Sciences. If his professional accomplishments do not impress you enough, he is also a renowned sword swallower. Please put your hands together and give a warm TED welcome to Dr. Hans Rosling! (Source: A completely fictitious introduction made up using Wikipedia information)*

Writing that nearly put me to sleep. In fact, I am going to keep a copy of that introduction on my night table as a cure for insomnia, and I recommend you do the same. By contrast, great introductions are more than a dry list of facts and accomplishments; great introductions present only facts relevant to the speaker's core message, are audience centric, and establish the speaker's credibility without placing him or her on a pedestal. Consider each of these qualities in turn.

Constructive introductions are limited in scope to information that ties to the speaker's central unifying idea. Dr. Rosling took the stage to inspire the influential TED Conference attendees to support the spread of free public health databases. That he earned his PhD in 1986 from Uppsala University for discovering and investigating an outbreak of a rare disease is admirable and amazing but not directly relevant to the core message of the talk. A better, on-point piece of information is that Dr. Rosling was chairman of the Karolinska International Research and Training Committee where he started health research collaborations with universities in Asia, Africa, the Middle East, and Latin America. That factoid provides a preview of what's to come, that the man about to take the stage has a passion for advancing public health through global partnerships.

TIP 108: Ensure that your introduction tells why you are the right person to share your idea with the audience.

A far more egregious flaw of the fake introduction in tip 107 is that it fails to tell the members of the audience what is in it for them. People do not sit for hours on end listening to other people speak unless they are going to get a return on their investment of time and attention. A great introduction tempts the audience with a taste of the benefit they are going to receive but does not go so far as to give away the bacon. A better introduction might have included something to the effect of "By the end of Hans's talk, you will learn the way that sharing global health data will enhance the quality of your life, the lives of your children, and the lives of 7 billion of your closest friends." With that small change, the audience has a reason to sit up and pay attention.

TIP 109: Craft an introduction that positions you as a credible guide, not as a superhuman.

Emcees must establish the speaker's credibility without making the person appear to be superhuman. Though we respect authority, we trust people who are more like us. We are inspired to alter our perspective and to rise to action by people just like us who started out as skeptics but succeeded after embracing change. The problem with the mock introduction in tip 107 is that it paints Dr. Rosling as a genius among geniuses. He is a statistician, a medical doctor, and an epidemiologist, and he has garnered countless accolades. Any person who hears this introduction will say, "Hans Rosling is amazing. But I can never do what he has done because I do not have his academic pedigree or his IQ." In this case, it is enough to say the following: "Dr. Rosling is professor of international health at Karolinska Institute and an important contributor to advancing the global discussion on public health." This is sufficient to establish the speaker's credibility and again ties directly to what he is about to discuss. Finally, the sword-swallowing bit humanizes the good doctor, but it does it in a circus-freak sort of way that is also not relevant to the topic at hand.

Most of the time, the person who introduces you will not know you from Adam. In that case, you should provide that person with a written introduction that follows the three tenets discussed here by sharing what is in it for the audience, by maximizing topical relevance, and by minimizing biographical information. Make sure to take the time to review the introduction with the emcee. If you have major concerns, you may respectfully ask him to practice it once or twice to get the timing and delivery down.

On the other hand, something magical happens when the emcee knows you even just a little; I discovered this firsthand. In 2011, I was invited to Portland to speak to 80 members of the entrepreneur peer-mentoring group StarveUps. My central theme was secrets to delivering presentations that help little companies close big company deals. Just before I went on stage, John Friess, a busy entrepreneur and the evening's emcee, admitted to me that he had neglected to review my introduction. Fortunately, we had gotten to know each other by speaking on the phone a few times before the event. He took a brief look at the copy I handed him, crumpled it up, put it in his pocket, and said, "Trust me." Needless to say, my blood pressure immediately rose more than a few points. John took the stage and proceeded to tell a brief personal story about his struggles with pitching to investors, partners, and customers. He then shared with the audience the story of how he met me and of my passion for trying to give everyone I meet the tools and the feedback needed to become inspiring communicators. I could not have asked for a better introduction.

TIP 110: Match the tone of your introduction to the tone of your speech.

The final consideration in crafting an introduction for your emcee is that the content should match the tone of your speech. I hope that the person who introduced Hans Rosling did not kick things off with a mini comedy routine. In contrast, a comic introduction is perfectly appropriate and highly desirable as a warm-up act for a funny speaker. The synchronization between the introduction and the speech helps manage the energy level in the room—something that will be discussed in the next chapter.

It is fairly standard for event organizers to ask you for a brief biography they can use to introduce you. The vast majority will simply read aloud what you provide, so use the tips in this chapter and then read what you wrote out loud to make sure it comes across as conversational. If the emcee deviates from the script, just shrug it off and move on.

Once the emcee starts the applause and shakes your hand, take a deep breath and have as much fun as you can during the next 18 minutes as you share your idea worth spreading.

CHAPTER 22

Helping Your TED Video Go Viral

TIP 111: Make your talk surprising, cute, creative, and emotional.

Professor Yoram Wind of the Wharton School at the University of Pennsylvania knows more than anybody else on the planet what it takes for videos to go viral. He figured out a recipe that improves the odds but does not guarantee that a video will generate millions of clicks on the Internet. Here is how he did it.

Professor Wind started with a list of the 73 most popular web advertising videos, according to the Visible Measures database. The videos ranged from 7 million to over 81 million views. He then paired each of the viral videos with a nonviral video that was as similar as possible. The pairs typically shared the same product brands and advertising agencies; they even had to be released within one year of each other. Next he tagged each video with one or more of the following 17 attributes:

Super Bowl	celebrities
call to action	humor
cause	cute
cocreation	sex
mascot	rational appeal
creative	emotional appeal
children	Facebook likes
animals	Twitter follower
surprise	

Finally, he ran the data through statistical analysis to determine which attributes predicted viral video sharing. He found only four attributes to be significant: surprise, cute, creative, and emotional appeal. With the possible exception of cute, the other three elements are found naturally in any TED Talk, so the key point is that you do not need to do anything special.

TIP 112: Let go of that which you cannot control.

I asked several TED speakers, including Richard St. John and Becky Blanton, what they did to make their videos go viral. The short answer is that they did not do anything. In Richard's case, he had millions of views before he even realized that his video was live on TED.com. In Becky's case, she had never seen her video in the nearly four years between the time she delivered her TED Talk and the time we spoke. I actually surprised her with the good news.

If you are already a celebrity like Amanda Palmer, Tony Robbins, or Malcolm Gladwell, then you will be able to promote the video to your millions of social media fans. For everyone else, share your best idea and then let it take flight on the winds of chance.

CHAPTER 23

Stop Reading and Start Speaking

TIP 113: Practice in a feedback-rich environment.

While writing this book, I studied TED videos. A lot of TED videos. In the same way that watching many episodes of *Iron Chef* will not make you a gourmet cook, watching many great speakers will not make you a great speaker. Reading a library of books on public speaking will not make you a great speaker either. The only way to conquer your fear and hone your speaking skills is to practice in a feedback-rich environment.

Go spread your ideas.

AFTERWORD

In order for our world to change for the better, great ideas need to spread. For ideas to spread, they must be easily understood. When they are easily understood, they become actionable. I wake up every day to inspire people to do the things that inspire them. We should strive to present our ideas in ways that will inspire others to join our movements or help champion our causes. The reason is simple; building something together is much more effective and more powerful than trying to build it alone.

When I speak, I never talk about things I do not understand or do not care about. I am not there to sell any products or services. If we do not care about the subject about which we are talking, then we should probably give a different talk. The more we care about the ideas we speak about, the more others will care about them too.

Before giving any talk, ask yourself, "Why am I giving this talk?" It is not enough to say you have invented something. It is not compelling to others simply to say you have a perspective on something you want to share. What is the reason you feel so compelled to give your message to others? What is so valuable that you would risk people disagreeing or even heckling you? What is so important that people should bother giving up any of their time to listen to you?

People often have the reasonably altruistic point of view, "If they learn this, then it will increase their productivity . . ." or something like that. However, the best TED Talks are grounded in the more deeply personal mindset, "I discovered or did something that dramatically changed my life. It was so powerful that I felt compelled to share it with others." Look at all of the 20 most viewed talks. Whether the speakers talk about their personal experience or not, the speeches are profoundly emotional for every single one of them. They either personally suffered or are intimately involved in whatever they are sharing. Watch Susan Cain's talk, for example (a favorite of mine), to see this in action.

The talk I gave was born from something deeply personal. It came from the time when I hit rock bottom. I lost my passion for what I was doing. During the struggle that I went through to regain my passion, I made the discovery that the most successful people and organizations on the planet always function on the same three levels—what we do, how we do it, and why we do it. The problem was that I only knew two of them. I knew what I did and was reasonably confident that I was good at it. I could explain how I was different from or better than my competition. But I could not say why I was doing it. My talk was not some commercial or academic exercise; it was an exercise to save myself. The discovery of this thing called 'The Why' profoundly changed my life. I shared it with my friends because that is what we do when we find something beautiful—we share it with the people we love. My friends, in turn, invited me to share it with their friends. People kept inviting me to share and share and share. I just kept saying yes. Even though I do not tell that story in my TEDx Talk, the speech I gave most certainly began out of something deeply, deeply personal. In other words, I really cared about what I was talking about.

If anything, I think people need to know what their strengths are and stick to them. I try and put myself in positions that will allow for me to be successful. TEDxPugetSound was no exception. I had already been giving extended versions of my talk for a few years and I knew the content inside and out. Plus I had been immersed in the subject because the book I was writing, *Start with Why*, was nearing publication. I trusted that I knew the content well enough that I could talk about it without notes.

People put so much pressure on themselves when they have an opportunity to give a TED and TEDx Talk. And I understand why. I am fully aware how a successful talk can significantly boost one's career. Given the potential upside, too many people become preoccupied with the production details that they sometimes miss what really matters—the message. I always remind people that the video and sound quality of my talk is pretty poor. And if that is not bad enough, while I was presenting, my wireless microphone failed and someone had to give me a new wired microphone. All of this was caught on camera. If your content is clear and well delivered, then people will overlook the production quality. If you panic because the wrong slide went up or your video did not play properly, the audience will also get distracted. For a talk to be successful, you must see yourself as the tour guide for an idea, not a stage manager for a production. And the best way to do that is to, again, focus on why you and the audience are there in the first place. It's not about you; it's about your message.

The single most important lesson I have learned is how to show up. You have to show up to give. Every time I speak, no matter who the audience is, I do not want anything from anybody. I do not want people's business. I do not want their approval. I do not want them to follow me on Twitter or Facebook. I do not want them to buy a book. I do not want anything. I show up to give; to share my thoughts, my opinions, my perspectives, and my ideas. I hold nothing back. I answer every question I am asked completely. I do not leave anything out so that they have to visit a website or sign up for a course. Doing those things represents a taking mentality. Showing up to give can make the difference between a brilliant and authentic speaker versus someone who is not.

A speaker may be rehearsed and polished, but if he or she shows up to get something from the audience, the talk often falls flat. I think a problem that has emerged from the TED experience is people now see it as their ticket to raise their profile, sell their book, or get more clients. However, if you show up to get, that will destroy any presentation you give. Fundamentally, it affects the way you present yourself because you will make it about you instead of your message and your audience. People are highly attuned social animals. We can always tell when someone wants to get something from us and when someone wants to genuinely give something to us with no expectation of anything in return . . . on or off the stage.

No matter the size of the audience, I think of the audience members as people I care about—people I want to spend my time sharing with. In the same vein, I am grateful for their time spent listening. I have a mantra that I actually say out loud to myself almost every time I go on stage, "You're here to give. You're here to share." I remind myself nearly every time why I am there. And when you do that, the reward you will receive is even greater.

I've learned, for example, that when you offer an audience an idea worth spreading, they will respond with excitement and gratitude. When you give them something powerful, they are often still thinking about it while they are clapping. And so they clap and clap and clap. You may have already exited the stage and yet they are still clapping. That is one of the greatest rewards I get; to see and hear and feel the impact I made.

On the day you give a TED or TEDx Talk, if the audience gives you a standing ovation or prolonged applause, then the odds are pretty high that people sitting at their desk will receive your message equally warmly.

I am often asked what I did, if anything, to help my video go viral. Jeremey touched on this, but I would like to elaborate. The whole concept of a virus is that it is an accident. No one can plan for something to go viral. And even when people do, even if they are successful, I can almost guarantee it is not for the reasons they think. If it was, they would be able to do it over and over and over, and they cannot. I giggle when companies sell services claiming to help your video go viral. We can work to create conditions in which a virus is more likely to spread, but there are no guarantees. It does not work that way. I meet many speakers with delusions of having their talks go viral using elaborate marketing plans to make it happen. Yet I do not know a single one that succeeded. If that's the goal, then it's the opposite of giving. That's showing up to take. The ideas that spread virally are the ones in which the speakers show up to give something expecting nothing in return. Those are the only ones that have a chance of going viral.

There are two big reasons my TEDx Talk about the concept of why did go viral. The main reason was luck. Keep in mind that when my TEDx Talk came out in September 2009, the TEDx franchise was still relatively new. Since there were so few talks online, the opportunity that mine would be seen was higher than it would be today. That was just dumb luck. The timing was good.

The other reason my TEDx video went viral, however, is that I did not do anything. I did not have a marketing plan. I did not have a publicist. There was no company overseas hitting "Like, Like, Like" on social networks. If there is some magic, it is that my message fundamentally resonated. I showed up to share something that means something to me personally—something I care deeply about. Something I would still be sharing just as passionately with my friends if there were no TED and there were no public speaking. For this reason, people could believe in it. And for those that did, just like I started by sharing it with my friends, they shared it with theirs. That is what makes ideas spread far and wide. It happened when others take it upon themselves to share. I have asked audiences, "How many of you have seen my TED Talk?" If a large number raise their hands, then I ask, "How many of you who have your hands raised were sent the talk by someone else?" The numbers are usually around 75 percent. Neither I nor any social media plan was the reason the video spread. It was because of all the amazing people who chose to share it.

When people perceive your message as so interesting, powerful, and valuable that they decide to send it to somebody they love, you become a vehicle for others to help their friends, their colleagues, or the ones they care about. We give beautiful things to the people we love. And if we see a movie, read a book, or hear a talk that touches us in some way, we share it with people we want to be touched in the same way. And so your ideas spread.

I'm starting to sound like a broken record by now, but if you show up to take, there is no reason for people to share your message because any information you gave them was selfishly motivated. They might even use it selfishly. "This was good. I'm keeping this one." However, if you show up to give, others will use your message in the same respect. That is fundamentally the reason why my message went viral. Others, by the grace of their generosity, were so kind as to share what I had to say with people they cared about.

I will leave you with this: Ideas alone do not change our world for the better. People do. Ideas that inspire people to act only start the process. When we share the ideas that inspire us in a way that inspires others to take action, then others will take it upon themselves to help build the world we imagine. And that's the best reason there is to share your ideas with all those who will listen.

—Simon Sinek,
New York Times bestselling author of *Start with Why*

NOTES

Foreword

1. St. John, Richard. "Richard St. John's 8 secrets of success." *TED2005*. TED Conferences LLC. <http://www.ted.com/talks/richard_st_john_s_8_secrets_of_success.html>.

Introduction

1. Robinson, Ken. "Schools kill creativity." *TED2006*. TED Conferences LLC. <http://www.ted.com/talks/ken_robinson_says_schools_kill_creativity.html>.

Chapter 1

1. Roy, Bunker. "Learning from a barefoot movement." *TEDGlobal 2011*. TED Conferences LLC. <http://www.ted.com/talks/bunker_roy.html>.
2. Gates, Bill. "Mosquitos, malaria and education." *TED2009*. TED Conferences LLC. <http://www.ted.com/talks/bill_gates_unplugged.html>.
3. Mistry, Pranav. "The thrilling potential of SixthSense technology." *TEDIndia 2009*. <http://www.ted.com/talks/pranav_mistry_the_thrilling_potential_of_sixthsense_technology.html>.
4. Thrun, Sebastian. "Google's driverless car." *TED2011*. TED Conferences LLC. <http://www.ted.com/talks/sebastian_thrun_google_s_driverless_car.html>.
5. Taylor, Jill Bolte. "Stroke of insight." *TED2008*. TED Conferences LLC. <http://www.ted.com/talks/jill_bolte_taylor_s_powerful_stroke_of_insight.html>.
6. Rosling, Hans. "Stats that reshape your worldview." *TED2006*. TED Conferences LLC. <http://www.ted.com/talks/hans_rosling_shows_the_best_stats_you_ve_ever_seen.html>.
7. de Grey, Aubrey. "A roadmap to end aging." *TEDGlobal 2005*. <http://www.ted.com/talks/aubrey_de_grey_says_we_can_avoid_aging.html>.
8. Greene, Brian. "Making sense of string theory." *TED2005*. TED Conferences LLC. <http://www.ted.com/talks/brian_greene_on_string_theory.html>.
9. Gallo, David. "Underwater astonishments." *TED2007*. TED Conferences LLC. <http://www.ted.com/talks/david_gallo_shows_underwater_astonishments.html>.

10. Hawking, Stephen. "Questioning the universe." *TED2008.* TED Conferences LLC. <http://www.ted.com/talks/stephen_hawking_asks_ big_questions_about_the_universe.html>.

11. Robinson, Ken. "Schools kill creativity." *TED2006.* TED Conferences LLC. <http://www.ted.com/talks/ken_robinson_says_schools_kill_creativity .html>.

12. Brown, Brené. "The power of vulnerability." *TEDxHouston 2010.* <http:// www.ted.com/talks/brene_brown_on_vulnerability.html>.

13. Silverman, Sarah. "A new perspective on the number 3000." *TED2010.* YouTube. <http://www.youtube.com/watch?v=ci5p1OdVLAc>.

14. Todd, Charlie. "The shared experience of absurdity." *TEDxBloomington 2011.* <http://www.ted.com/talks/charlie_todd_the_shared_experience_ of_absurdity.html>.

15. Frank, Ze. "Nerdcore comedy." *TED2004.* TED Conferences LLC. <http:// www.ted.com/talks/ze_frank_s_nerdcore_comedy.html>.

16. Watts, Reggie. "Reggie Watts disorients you in the most entertaining way." *TED2012.* TED Conferences LLC. <http://www.ted.com/talks/reggie_ watts_disorients_you_in_the_most_entertaining_way.html>.

17. Jobrani, Maz. "Did you hear the one about the Iranian-American?" *TEDGlobal 2010.* TED Conferences LLC. <http://www.ted.com/talks/maz_ jobrani_make_jokes_not_bombs.html>.

18. Benjamin, Arthur. "Mathemagic." *TED2005.* TED Conferences LLC. <http://www.ted.com/talks/arthur_benjamin_does_mathemagic.html>.

19. Barry, Keith. "Brain magic." *TED2004.* TED Conferences LLC. <http:// www.ted.com/talks/keith_barry_does_brain_magic.html>.

20. Tempest, Marco. "Augmented reality, techno-magic." *TEDGlobal 2011.* TED Conferences LLC. <http://www.ted.com/talks/marco_tempest_the_ augmented_reality_of_techno_magic.html>.

21. Randi, James. "Homeopathy, quackery and fraud." *TED2007.* TED Conferences LLC. <http://www.ted.com/talks/james_randi.html>.

22. Gilbert, Elizabeth. "Your elusive creative genius." *TED2009.* TED Conferences LLC. <http://www.ted.com/talks/elizabeth_gilbert_on_ genius.html>.

23. Adichie, Chimamanda. "The danger of a single story." *TEDGlobal 2009.* TED Conferences LLC. <http://www.ted.com/talks/chimamanda_adichie_ the_danger_of_a_single_story.html>.

24. Allende, Isabel. "Tales of passion." *TED2007.* TED Conferences LLC. <http://www.ted.com/talks/isabel_allende_tells_tales_of_passion.html>.

25. Walker, Karen Thompson. "What fear can teach us." *TEDGlobal 2012.* TED Conferences LLC. <http://www.ted.com/talks/karen_thompson_walker_ what_fear_can_teach_us.html>.

26. Zander, Benjamin. "The transformative power of classical music." *TED2008.* TED Conferences LLC. <http://www.ted.com/talks/benjamin_ zander_on_music_and_passion.html>.

27. Chang, Candy. "Before I die I want to . . ." *TEDGlobal 2012.* TED Conferences LLC. <http://www.ted.com/talks/candy_chang_before_i_ die_i_want_to.html>.

28. Johansson, Erik. "Impossible photography." *TEDSalon London Fall 2011.* TED Conferences LLC. <http://www.ted.com/talks/erik_johansson_impossible_photography.html>.
29. Lotto, Beau. "Optical illusions show how we see." *TEDGlobal 2009.* TED Conferences LLC. <http://www.ted.com/talks/beau_lotto_optical_illusions_show_how_we_see.html>.
30. Oliver, Jamie. "Teach every child about food." *TED2010.* TED Conferences LLC. <http://www.ted.com/talks/jamie_oliver.html>.
31. Grandin, Temple. "The world needs all kinds of minds." *TED2010.* TED Conferences LLC. <http://www.ted.com/talks/temple_grandin_the_world_needs_all_kinds_of_minds.html>.
32. Sutherland, Rory. "Life lessons from an ad man." *TEDGlobal 2009.* <http://www.ted.com/talks/rory_sutherland_life_lessons_from_an_ad_man.html>.
33. Russell, Cameron. "Looks aren't everything. Believe me, I'm a model." *TEDxMidAtlantic 2012.* <http://www.ted.com/talks/cameron_russell_looks_aren_t_everything_believe_me_i_m_a_model.html>.
34. Van Uhm, Peter. "Why I chose a gun." *TEDxAmsterdam 2011.* <http://www.ted.com/talks/peter_van_uhm_why_i_chose_a_gun.html>.
35. Sandberg, Sheryl. "Why we have too few women leaders." *TEDWomen 2010.* TED Conferences LLC. <http://www.ted.com/talks/sheryl_sandberg_why_we_have_too_few_women_leaders.html>.
36. Sinek, Simon. "How great leaders inspire action." *TEDxPuget Sound 2009.* <http://www.ted.com/talks/simon_sinek_how_great_leaders_inspire_action.html>.
37. Pink, Dan. "The puzzle of motivation." *TEDGlobal 2009.* TED Conferences LLC. <http://www.ted.com/talks/dan_pink_on_motivation.html>.
38. Godin, Seth. "How to get your ideas to spread." *TED2003.* TED Conferences LLC. <http://www.ted.com/talks/seth_godin_on_sliced_bread.html>.
39. Elias, Ric. "3 things I learned while my plane crashed." *TED2011.* TED Conferences LLC. <http://www.ted.com/talks/ric_elias.html>.
40. Gavagan, Ed. "A story about knots and surgeons." *TEDMED 2012.* TED Conferences LLC. <http://www.ted.com/talks/ed_gavagan_a_story_about_knots_and_surgeons.html>.
41. Cutts, Matt. "Try something new for 30 days." *TED2011.* TED Conferences LLC. <http://www.ted.com/talks/matt_cutts_try_something_new_for_30_days.html>.
42. Smith, Joe. "How to use a paper towel." *TEDxConcordiaUPortland 2012.* <http://www.ted.com/talks/joe_smith_how_to_use_a_paper_towel.html>.
43. Robbins, Tony. "Why we do what we do." *TED2006.* TED Conferences LLC. <http://www.ted.com/talks/tony_robbins_asks_why_we_do_what_we_do.html>.
44. Gladwell, Malcolm. "Choice, happiness and spaghetti sauce." *TED2004.* TED Conferences LLC. <http://www.ted.com/talks/malcolm_gladwell_on_spaghetti_sauce.html>.

45. Roach, Mary. "10 things you didn't know about orgasm." *TED2009*. TED Conferences LLC. <http://www.ted.com/talks/mary_roach_10_things_you_didn_t_know_about_orgasm.html>.

46. Cain, Susan. "The power of introverts." *TED2012*. TED Conferences LLC. <http://www.ted.com/talks/susan_cain_the_power_of_introverts.html>.

47. Gutman, Ron. "The hidden power of smiling." *TED2011*. TED Conferences LLC. <http://www.ted.com/talks/ron_gutman_the_hidden_power_of_smiling.html>.

48. Khan, Salman. "Let's use video to reinvent education." *TED2011*. TED Conferences LLC. <http://www.ted.com/talks/salman_khan_let_s_use_video_to_reinvent_education.html>.

49. McGonigal, Jane. "Gaming can make a better world." *TED2010*. TED Conferences LLC. <http://www.ted.com/talks/jane_mcgonigal_gaming_can_make_a_better_world.html>.

50. Pritchard , Michael. "How to make filthy water drinkable." *TEDGlobal 2009*. TED Conferences LLC. <http://www.ted.com/talks/michael_pritchard_invents_a_water_filter.html>.

51. Stamets, Paul. "6 ways mushrooms can save the world." *TED2008*. TED Conferences LLC. <http://www.ted.com/talks/paul_stamets_on_6_ways_mushrooms_can_save_the_world.html>.

52. Fisher, Helen. "The brain in love." *TED2008*. TED Conferences LLC. <http://www.ted.com/talks/helen_fisher_studies_the_brain_in_love.html>.

Chapter 2

1. Taylor, Jill Bolte. "Stroke of insight." *TED2008*. TED Conferences LLC. <http://www.ted.com/talks/jill_bolte_taylor_s_powerful_stroke_of_insight.html>.

2. Todd, Charlie. "The shared experience of absurdity." *TEDxBloomington 2011*. <http://www.ted.com/talks/charlie_todd_the_shared_experience_of_absurdity.html>.

3. Cutts, Matt. "Try something new for 30 days." *TED2011*. TED Conferences LLC. <http://www.ted.com/talks/matt_cutts_try_something_new_for_30_days.html>.

4. Roy, Bunker. "Learning from a barefoot movement." *TEDGlobal 2011*. TED Conferences LLC. <http://www.ted.com/talks/bunker_roy.html>.

5. Cain, Susan. "The power of introverts." *TED2012*. TED Conferences LLC. <http://www.ted.com/talks/susan_cain_the_power_of_introverts.html>.

6. Khan, Salman. "Let's use video to reinvent education." *TED2011*. TED Conferences LLC. <http://www.ted.com/talks/salman_khan_let_s_use_video_to_reinvent_education.html>.

7. Robinson, Ken. "Schools kill creativity." *TED2006*. TED Conferences LLC. <http://www.ted.com/talks/ken_robinson_says_schools_kill_creativity.html>.

Chapter 3

1. Steiner, Leslie Morgan. "Why domestic violence victims don't leave." *TEDxRainier 2012.* <http://www.ted.com/talks/leslie_morgan_steiner_why_domestic_violence_victims_don_t_leave.html>.
2. Blanton, Becky. "The year I was homeless." *TEDGlobal 2009.* TED Conferences LLC. <http://www.ted.com/talks/becky_blanton_the_year_i_was_homeless.html>.
3. Gladwell, Malcolm. "Choice, happiness and spaghetti sauce." *TED2004.* TED Conferences LLC. <http://www.ted.com/talks/malcolm_gladwell_on_spaghetti_sauce.html>.
4. Taylor, Jill Bolte. "Stroke of insight." *TED2008.* TED Conferences LLC. <http://www.ted.com/talks/jill_bolte_taylor_s_powerful_stroke_of_insight.html>.
5. Russell, Cameron. "Looks aren't everything. Believe me, I'm a model." *TEDxMidAtlantic 2012.* <http://www.ted.com/talks/cameron_russell_looks_aren_t_everything_believe_me_i_m_a_model.html>.

Chapter 4

1. Sinek, Simon. "How great leaders inspire action." *TEDxPugetSound 2009.* <http://www.ted.com/talks/simon_sinek_how_great_leaders_inspire_action.html>.

Chapter 5

1. Robinson, Ken. "Schools kill creativity." *TED2006.* TED Conferences LLC. <http://www.ted.com/talks/ken_robinson_says_schools_kill_creativity.html>.
2. Roy, Deb. "The birth of a word." *TED2011.* TED Conferences LLC. <http://www.ted.com/talks/deb_roy_the_birth_of_a_word.html>.
3. St. John, Richard. "Richard St. John's 8 secrets of success." *TED2005.* TED Conferences LLC. <http://www.ted.com/talks/richard_st_john_s_8_secrets_of_success.html>.
4. Oliver, Jamie. "Teach every child about food." *TED2010.* TED Conferences LLC. <http://www.ted.com/talks/jamie_oliver.html>.
5. Sinek, Simon. "How great leaders inspire action." *TEDxPuget Sound 2009.* <http://www.ted.com/talks/simon_sinek_how_great_leaders_inspire_action.html>.
6. Thomashauer, Regena. "The pleasure revolution." *TEDxFiDiWomen 2011.* <http://www.youtube.com/watch?v=CU9RAGiRdSE>.

Chapter 6

1. Adichie, Chimamanda. "The danger of a single story." *TEDGlobal 2009.* TED Conferences LLC. <http://www.ted.com/talks/chimamanda_adichie_the_danger_of_a_single_story.html>.

Chapter 7

1. Brown, Brené. "The power of vulnerability." *TEDxHouston 2010.* <http://www.ted.com/talks/brene_brown_on_vulnerability.html>.
2. Zander, Benjamin. "The transformative power of classical music." *TED2008.* TED Conferences LLC. <http://www.ted.com/talks/benjamin_zander_on_music_and_passion.html>.
3. Roy, Bunker. "Learning from a barefoot movement." *TEDGlobal 2011.* TED Conferences LLC. <http://www.ted.com/talks/bunker_roy.html>.
4. Russell, Cameron. "Looks aren't everything. Believe me, I'm a model." *TEDxMidAtlantic 2012.* <http://www.ted.com/talks/cameron_russell_looks_aren_t_everything_believe_me_i_m_a_model.html>.
5. Roy, Deb. "The birth of a word." *TED2011.* TED Conferences LLC. <http://www.ted.com/talks/deb_roy_the_birth_of_a_word.html>.
6. Oliver, Jamie. "Teach every child about food." *TED2010.* TED Conferences LLC. <http://www.ted.com/talks/jamie_oliver.html>.
7. Taylor, Jill Bolte. "Stroke of insight." *TED2008.* TED Conferences LLC. <http://www.ted.com/talks/jill_bolte_taylor_s_powerful_stroke_of_insight.html>.
8. St. John, Richard. "Richard St. John's 8 secrets of success." *TED2005.* TED Conferences LLC. <http://www.ted.com/talks/richard_st_john_s_8_secrets_of_success.html>.
9. Sutherland, Rory. "Life lessons from an ad man." *TEDGlobal 2009.* <http://www.ted.com/talks/rory_sutherland_life_lessons_from_an_ad_man.html>.
10. Khan, Salman. "Let's use video to reinvent education." *TED2011.* TED Conferences LLC. <http://www.ted.com/talks/salman_khan_let_s_use_video_to_reinvent_education.html>.
11. Cain, Susan. "The power of introverts." *TED2012.* TED Conferences LLC. <http://www.ted.com/talks/susan_cain_the_power_of_introverts.html>.
12. Walker, Karen Thompson. "What fear can teach us." *TEDGlobal 2012.* TED Conferences LLC. <http://www.ted.com/talks/karen_thompson_walker_what_fear_can_teach_us.html>.

Chapter 8

1. Palmer, Amanda. "The art of asking." *TED2013.* TED Conferences LLC. <http://www.ted.com/talks/amanda_palmer_the_art_of_asking.html>.
2. Chen, Jane. "A warm embrace that saves lives." *TEDIndia 2009.* TED Conferences LLC. <http://www.ted.com/talks/jane_chen_a_warm_embrace_that_saves_lives.html>.
3. Taylor, Jill Bolte. "Stroke of insight." *TED2008.* TED Conferences LLC. <http://www.ted.com/talks/jill_bolte_taylor_s_powerful_stroke_of_insight.html>.
4. Elias, Ric. "3 things I learned while my plane crashed." *TED2011.* TED Conferences LLC. <http://www.ted.com/talks/ric_elias.html>.

Chapter 9

1. Cuddy, Amy. "Your body language shapes who you are." *TEDGlobal 2012.* TED Conferences LLC. <http://www.ted.com/talks/amy_cuddy_your_body_language_shapes_who_you_are.html>.

Chapter 10

1. Rosling, Hans. "Stats that reshape your worldview." *TED2006.* TED Conferences LLC. <http://www.ted.com/talks/hans_rosling_shows_the_best_stats_you_ve_ever_seen.html>.
2. Robinson, Ken. "Schools kill creativity." *TED2006.* TED Conferences LLC. <http://www.ted.com/talks/ken_robinson_says_schools_kill_creativity.html>.
3. Elias, Ric. "3 things I learned while my plane crashed." *TED2011.* TED Conferences LLC. <http://www.ted.com/talks/ric_elias.html>.
4. Taylor, Jill Bolte. "Stroke of insight." *TED2008.* TED Conferences LLC. <http://www.ted.com/talks/jill_bolte_taylor_s_powerful_stroke_of_insight.html>.

Chapter 11

1. Jobs, Steve. "How to live before you die." *Stanford University 2005 Commencement Address.* <http://www.ted.com/talks/steve_jobs_how_to_live_before_you_die.html>.

Chapter 13

1. Pink, Dan. "The puzzle of motivation." *TEDGlobal 2009.* TED Conferences LLC. <http://www.ted.com/talks/dan_pink_on_motivation.html>.

Chapter 14

1. Robinson, Ken. "Schools kill creativity." *TED2006.* TED Conferences LLC. <http://www.ted.com/talks/ken_robinson_says_schools_kill_creativity.html>.
2. Sinek, Simon. "How great leaders inspire action." *TEDxPuget Sound 2009.* <http://www.ted.com/talks/simon_sinek_how_great_leaders_inspire_action.html>.
3. Godin, Seth. "How to get your ideas to spread." *TED2003.* TED Conferences LLC. <http://www.ted.com/talks/seth_godin_on_sliced_bread.html>.
4. Godin, Seth. "The tribes we lead." *TED2009.* TED Conferences LLC. <http://www.ted.com/talks/seth_godin_on_the_tribes_we_lead.html>.

Chapter 15

1. Sutherland, Rory. "Life lessons from an ad man." *TEDGlobal 2009.* <http://www.ted.com/talks/rory_sutherland_life_lessons_from_an_ad_man.html>.

2. Todd, Charlie. "The shared experience of absurdity." *TEDxBloomington 2011.* <http://www.ted.com/talks/charlie_todd_the_shared_experience_of_absurdity.html>.

Chapter 16

1. Roy, Bunker. "Learning from a barefoot movement." *TEDGlobal 2011.* TED Conferences LLC. <http://www.ted.com/talks/bunker_roy.html>.
2. Mistry, Pranav. "The thrilling potential of SixthSense technology." *TEDIndia 2009.* <http://www.ted.com/talks/pranav_mistry_the_thrilling_potential_of_sixthsense_technology.html>.
3. Fischer, Markus. "A robot that flies like a bird." *TEDGlobal 2011.* TED Conferences LLC. <http://www.ted.com/talks/a_robot_that_flies_like_a_bird.html>.

Chapter 17

1. Adichie, Chimamanda. "The danger of a single story." *TEDGlobal 2009.* TED Conferences LLC. <http://www.ted.com/talks/chimamanda_adichie_the_danger_of_a_single_story.html>.
2. Walker, Karen Thompson. "What fear can teach us." *TEDGlobal 2012.* TED Conferences LLC. <http://www.ted.com/talks/karen_thompson_walker_what_fear_can_teach_us.html>.

Chapter 18

1. Roy, Bunker. "Learning from a barefoot movement." *TEDGlobal 2011.* TED Conferences LLC. <http://www.ted.com/talks/bunker_roy.html>.
2. Palmer, Amanda. "The art of asking." *TED2013.* TED Conferences LLC. <http://www.ted.com/talks/amanda_palmer_the_art_of_asking.html>.
3. Robinson, Ken. "Schools kill creativity." *TED2006.* TED Conferences LLC. <http://www.ted.com/talks/ken_robinson_says_schools_kill_creativity.html>.

Chapter 19

1. Blanton, Becky. "The year I was homeless." *TEDGlobal 2009.* TED Conferences LLC. <http://www.ted.com/talks/becky_blanton_the_year_i_was_homeless.html>.
2. St. John, Richard. "Richard St. John's 8 secrets of success." *TED2005.* TED Conferences LLC. <http://www.ted.com/talks/richard_st_john_s_8_secrets_of_success.html>.
3. Gallop, Cindy. "Make love, not porn." *TED2009.* TED Conferences LLC. <http://www.youtube.com/watch?v=FV8n_E_6Tpc>.

INDEX

ABOUT THE AUTHOR

Jeremey Donovan is group vice president of marketing at Gartner, Inc., the world's leading information technology research and advisory company with $1.6 billion in annual revenue. During his career, Jeremey has led successful teams focused on market research, new product development, marketing, acquisitions, and product management. He is a three-time TEDx organizer, a TEDx speaker, a coach for many TED and TEDx speakers, and a long-time member of Toastmasters International. His other books include *What Great Looks Like* and *How to Win the Toastmasters World Championship of Public Speaking*.